soup

soup

BY NICK SANDLER
AND JOHNNY ACTON

PHOTOGRAPHY BY
GEORGIA GLYNN SMITH

whitecap

DEDICATION

to Monsieur Boulanger, the spiritual godfather of the Soup Bar

This edition published in Canada by Whitecap Books Limited

For more information, please contact

Whitecap Books

351 Lynn Avenue,

North Vancouver, British Columbia,

Canada V7J 2C4

www.whitecap.ca

First published in 1999 by Kyle Cathie Limited

Reprinted 2003

10 9 8 7 6 5 4 3 2 1

ISBN 1 55285 554 6

Edited by Alexa Stace

Designed by Gavin Pretor-Pinney

Production by Lorraine Baird and Sha Huxtable

Home Economy by Linda Tubby

Colour separation by Colourscan, Singapore

Printed and bound by Tien Wah Press, Singapore

Contents

Preface

If we are qualified 'Soup Doctors'. SOUP works was our university. For two glorious years, starting in November 1998, this spirited mini-chain offered discerning punters in London's Soho and Covent Garden an alternative to the ubiquitous lunchtime sandwich. Our philosophy was simple: to produce a delicious, international range of fresh soups and stews to meet what we wagered was a vast dormant demand for these universal and versatile foods. And from day one, with the queue snaking out into the street, we saw our hunch being confirmed again and again.

Something about soup seemed to have captured the zeitgeist. Maybe it was to do with its healthiness. Perhaps it was its truly global nature - the world in a bowl, as one of our slogans would have it. Since those heady days, things have moved on. SOUP works, per se, no longer exists. But the fashion for quality fresh soup continues to gather momentum. It is ubiquitous in cafés and restaurants. Supermarkets are heaving with the stuff. Still, it's much more satisfying to make your own.

This book is written in the hope of transmitting the excitement and sense of adventure with which we entered the never-ending universe of soups, together with any savvy we've managed to acquire since. We view soup-making as a kind of alchemy: the blending of often very simple ingredients to produce something greater by far than the sum of its parts. Using this book, we hope that you too will be inspired to become an alchemist.

Introduction

SOUP is the food of the world. Every culture produces its own delicious variations on this universal theme, from the frozen wastes of Greenland (where one of your authors experienced a seal soup most charitably described as 'interesting') to the noodle stalls of Bangkok. Soup has a history as old as civilization, yet always manages, through its continual evolution and inexhaustible versatility, to appear at the cutting edge of contemporary cooking. It is comforting and familiar, but can at the same time be exotic and exciting. It offers a permanent invitation to improvisation and embellishment. Finally, soup is exceptionally healthy, with a proven ability to aid dieting, and is remarkably easy to make. It is, in short, pretty good stuff.

This book is unlike any other that we are aware of because it approaches the subject of soup geographically, emphasizing the truly global nature of this wonder food. This seems particularly appropriate for an era in which everyone has become something of a 'gastronaut'. Even those who would have felt nervous in the company of an avocado a generation ago are now regularly tucking into Oriental, Mexican and Middle Eastern food. Supermarket shelves are bulging with multi-cultural goodies. No food better reflects this diversity than soup, and none is more accessible.

In each of the regions we cover, soup is almost literally a distillation of the relevant eating culture. This is one of the reasons we love it so much. Thus Chinese soups are characterized by harmonious balance of yin and yang elements, Japanese soups tend to place great emphasis on aesthetic presentation, and Mexican soups are dominated by the local staples of beans and chillies. Every region has its archetypal flavours, and flavour is what good soup-making is all about.

In case this all sounds a little intimidating, we would like to reassure you that most of the recipes in this book do not require outlandish ingredients or complex cooking techniques. We have set out, above all, to impart the spirit of good soup-making – an understanding of flavour and a willingness to experiment, rather than a slavish adherence to set recipes (although, recognizing that some people quite like to cook 'by numbers', we give you that option too).

One of our most successful soups, Polish Blueberry, came into being simply because one day Nick couldn't find the sour cherries he needed for a certain Hungarian recipe. So he improvised. We only learned much later that an obscure Polish recipe for Blueberry soup had existed all along! The moral of the story is that with a little imagination and a grasp of the essentials of soup making, you can't really go wrong.

THE HISTORY OF SOUP

Life itself began with soup. Scientists have long known the cocktail of organic chemicals which sloshed around in the seas of the young earth as the 'primordial soup' and it was from this that the first strands of DNA emerged, around 2 billion years ago. However, despite the best efforts of would-be Dr Frankensteins, the recipe has thus far proved elusive.

When *homo sapiens* eventually appeared on the scene, he seemed in a desperate hurry to get back to his roots. Archaeological evidence reveals that primitive man was preparing soup before he had even developed pots sturdy enough in which to cook the stuff. Instead, he improvised, dropping red hot stones into fragile clay pots filled with liquid gruel to heat it up.

Things improved, at least in the UK, with the arrival of migrants from Northern France in the fourth millenium BC bringing not only the basic ingredients for early soup (cultivated wheat and barley plus sheep and goats), but also decent pottery to boil it in. This allowed the release of starch from cereals into the liquid, bringing about the all important 'soupy' texture.

Not that all Iron Age soup recipes were any great shakes by modern standards. When the version found in the stomach of Denmark's celebrated Tolland Man was recreated for a BBC documentary in 1954, the two presenters who tried it almost brought it straight back up.

The next major development was the introduction of the bronze cooking pot or cauldron, which was suitable for cooking meat, an option which did wonders for the menu. So important were these vessels to Bronze Age man that he invested them with mystical qualities, the origin of the widespread association between cauldrons and witchcraft. Bizarrely, he also took to chucking them in lakes, probably an attempt to persuade the resident nature gods to keep earthly cauldrons well filled.

Meanwhile, in the Middle East, according to the Book of Genesis, the entire course of Jewish history was altered by a bowl of soup. One day, Esau returned empty handed from a day's hunting and sold his birthright to his younger and more stay-at-home twin brother Jacob just for the sake of a particularly good bowl of lentil pottage. Biblical scholars have interpreted the story as an allegory of the triumph of agriculture over the hunter-gatherer way of life. What is certain is that Jacob, not Esau, became the father of the Jews.

Back in Britain, the arrival of the Romans in the Second Century AD brought all kinds of goodies with which to sweeten the pot, including leeks, onions, carrots, fennel, mint, thyme, parsley and coriander. Their soups tended to be complex and faintly alarming affairs, as the oldest surviving recipe in the world (from Apicus' Fourth Century cookbook) makes clear. Called 'Pultes Iulianae', or 'Julian Pottage', it included wheat gruel, mincemeat, brains, wine, lovage, fennelseed and a good splash of fermented fish sauce.

The hasty departure of the Romans in the early Fifth Century plunged British soup making into Dark Age obscurity. The only surviving soup recipes from the Anglo-Saxon period are for medicinal pottages, such as a concoction of barley meal, shredded radish, herbs and salt stewed in butter prescribed for lung complaints. What is clear, however, is that this was the period in which porridge, soup's first cousin, came to dominate the scene, particularly in colder and wetter upland areas.

After the Norman Conquest, the status of soup picked up considerably. Spicy broths and pottages became an important part of the noble diet, in the form of a bewildering array of civeys, graveys, bukkenades and egerdouces. Many of these were derived from Saracen dishes picked up during the Crusades, such as the several thick smooth 'standing' pottages referred to in a cookery book dating from around 1325. The most famous of these was the original blancmange.

Andrew Boorde, writing in 1598, describes something nearer the modern concept of soup, which he claims was eaten throughout the England of his day: 'Pottage is made of the lyquor in which flessche is sodden in, with putting to chopped herbes and oatmeal and salt'. The presence of meat in this recipe is an indication of the growth of prosperity during the Tudor and Elizabethan periods. During the same era, new ingredients from the Americas (the tomato and the potato) began to arrive which would ultimately change the face of soup for ever.

During the seventeenth century, the dominant position of soups, stews and their relatives on the tables of Western Europe came under threat from a number of directions, including a sudden craze for cereal puddings baked in cloth and a new vogue for boiled and buttered vegetable side dishes. But most ominous of all was the growing popularity of that demonic new invention, the table fork. Before, food had needed to be spoonable by default. Now this was no longer the case, and all kinds of rival foodstuffs began to emerge to fill the vacuum. But just as soup looked to be on the way out, a fashion for a thinner type of pottage arrived from France to save the day. It had acquired the name 'soupe' from the practice of placing a 'sop' of bread at the bottom of bowls of pottage to soak up the juices. The sop itself soon disappeared, but the name lived on. Soup in the modern sense had arrived.

The following century saw the developments of stock cubes, like the 'portable soup' Captain Cook fortified himself with on his round the world voyage of 1772, made by evaporating clarified beef broth until it reached the consistency of glue. Still more significant, particularly from our point of view, was the opening of M Boulanger's soup shop in Paris in 1765. This august establishment was nothing less than the world's very first restaurant, and critically, it sold nothing but soup. The name 'restaurant' came from a sign hung over the door which read *'Boulanger vends les restaurants magiques'* (Boulanger sells magic restoratives). As they say, what goes around comes around…

The story of soup since M Boulanger's day has been dominated by the somewhat soulless techniques of mass production. Canning and powdering may not have done much for the palate, but they have certainly made for convenience and big business. Campbell's tinned soups in particular received the ultimate endorsement as American cultural icon through Andy Warhol's 1960s silkscreens. But lest the magnates grow complacent, slumbering hunger for the real thing was about to erupt in a fresh soup revolution. In the mid 1980s, a cantankerous genius named Al Yeganeh started selling sublime fresh soups from a hatch in midtown Manhattan. Cult status and a parody in the hit comedy *Seinfeld* followed, and suddenly gourmet soup bars were springing up everywhere.

And then we came along…

Western Europe

IF YOU WANT to know what is really important in a culture, look at its myths and folk stories. In Western Europe, one fairy tale in particular stands out for our purposes, and that is the story of Stone Soup. There are numerous versions, but the basics go something like this:

One day a man arrives in a village claiming to possess a magic stone with which he can make the most fantastic soup. All he needs, he tells the hungry villagers, is to put it in a cauldron of boiling water. This is rustled up in no time, in goes the stone and everyone gathers round expectantly. 'I can't help noticing that lovely bunch of onions in the corner,' says the hero. 'If I could just borrow one or two, it would make the soup even better.' Everyone agrees enthusiastically. 'Now I mention it, a few of those carrots wouldn't go amiss either,' he adds. Enter the carrots. 'I don't suppose that old chicken carcass is going begging?' he says after a few minutes. Before long he has pretty much emptied the larder, but when he whips out the stone and serves up the best soup anyone present has ever tasted, the villagers are gullible and helpful enough to put it all down to the magic stone. No doubt the hero gets to marry the king's daughter and live happily ever after too.

What this story actually means is an open question. Perhaps it is an endorsement of the alchemy theme we mentioned in the introduction. Maybe it is saying 'People are suckers and they want to believe in magic' or 'Great things can come from the most unpromising beginnings'. On the whole, we prefer to let it stand as a sweet bit of early soup propaganda. But it does unquestionably demonstrate the importance of soup in the folk memory of Western Europe.

While we're on this theme, mention should be made of a couple of choice European proverbs – 'Who soups long lives long' from Germany and, 'Of soup and love the first is the best' from Spain. Also worthy of the most careful attention is the cautionary tale of Augustus in *Shock-Headed Peter*, a German children's book which has been freaking out children since Victorian times. Initially a chubby lad, Augustus rejects his yummy soup and wastes away to nothing within days. Serves him right, we say. Even Beethoven got in on the act, memorably declaring that 'Only the pure in heart can make a good soup'.

The actual character of the soups of Western Europe varies from country to country, according to local tastes and produce. You will not be surprised, therefore, to find dill and salmon featuring prominently in Scandinavian soups, or sausages in German ones. French soups tend to be cultured and classical, while British soups often have a 'garden of England' quality. Atlantic seafood is well represented, and seasonal variations are prominent. Beyond that, it is just a matter of grabbing a ladle and diving in.

CONSOMMÉ

A good consommé should mean as much to the British as a fine broth does to the people of Japan. It certainly did in the Victorian and Edwardian eras. But somewhere the art of making this clear amber essence-of-an-essence has been lost. Perhaps we've all just grown too impatient. The only consommé on sale out there is in cans, and it's not always that great, which is why we've included a recipe for this neglected classic.

1.7 litres/2¾ pints chilled beef stock (see page 148)
700g/1¾lb minced beef, the leaner the better
70g/2¾oz onion, finely chopped
180g egg white (approx. 6 eggs)
1 large sprig flat-leaf parsley, finely chopped
1 sprig thyme, finely chopped
½tbs Worcester sauce
40ml/1½fl oz port
50ml/2fl oz dry sherry
30ml/1¼fl oz Madeira
A pinch of salt
A pinch of ground cloves
1½tbs mirin (sweetish Japanese cooking sherry)
1½tbs soy sauce

SERVES 6-8 [L][G]

• Take all the ingredients apart from the beef stock and mix together thoroughly in a large bowl.
• Make sure the beef stock has been well chilled before use. Pour into a large saucepan then stir in the rest of the ingredients.
• Slowly heat the consommé until simmering. Stir occasionally at first, but once the egg white starts to set, do not touch the liquid anymore. This will allow the albumen to do its work, cleansing the consommé of any impurities. Leave it to simmer undisturbed for 40 minutes, but do not allow to come to a full boil.
• Assuming you don't possess a stockpot with a tap at the base, which would make the job laughably easy, you'll now need to strain the liquid through a muslin. Gently tip the pan to one side, keeping the solid ingredients (which should have congealed into a solid mass) from spilling out with a spatula or similar implement.
• Serve immediately as a starter or inter-course tonic.
(The consommé will keep in the fridge for a few days and can also be frozen)

STRAWBERRY

This is the last word in hedonism, providing you are very careful about the quality of the strawberries you use. Only naturally ripened ones will really do – imported ones tend to be bland and sour. Wild strawberries are even better. Nick managed to transplant some into his garden, where they are now threatening to colonise the whole neighbourhood.

800g/1¾lb strawberries
75ml/3fl oz freshly squeezed orange juice
75ml/3fl oz white wine
125g/4oz honey, adjustable according to sweetness of the strawberries
2 tbs cornflour
50ml/2fl oz cold water
a squirt of lemon juice
chopped strawberries to garnish (ideally wild ones)

• Blend the strawberries and pass them through a fine sieve to remove the seeds.
• Combine the strawberries, orange juice, white wine and honey in a saucepan and stir until the honey dissolves over a low to medium flame.
• Beat the cornflour into the water with a fork or a mini-whisk and pour this mixture into the simmering soup. Stir until the soup thickens, which will take a few minutes. Add the lemon juice.
• Garnish with chopped strawberries.
MAKES 6-8 SMALL PORTIONS [D][V]

ASPARAGUS AND GRUYERE

Gruyère is quite a strong cheese with a distinctive, pungent taste. Asparagus, meanwhile, is a delicate vegetable with a magical, deep, mellow taste. So what are they doing together in a soup? Well, they don't have any choice, because Nick puts them there regularly, and to great effect.

600g/1¼lb asparagus
50g/2oz butter
125g/4oz shallots, chopped
125g/4oz celery, chopped
125g/4oz leeks, chopped
1.25 litres/2 pints Chicken Stock (see page 147)
50g/2oz plain flour
250g/8oz Gruyère, grated
200ml/7fl oz double cream
1 tbs chopped fresh tarragon

• Trim the bottoms of the asparagus stalks, then cut each stalk in two. Slice the asparagus stalks into 1cm/½in sections, and reserve the tip sections in a bowl
• Melt the butter in a large pan over gentle heat. Add the shallots, celery and leeks, cover and sweat until soft. Meanwhile, heat up the stock in a separate pan.
• Stir the flour into the vegetables, then add the stock and asparagus stalks and simmer for 10 minutes. Add the Gruyère and blend in a food processor. Return the soup to the pan, add the asparagus tips and simmer for 5 minutes. Pour in the cream, simmer briefly to bring the soup back up to temperature, and serve sprinkled with tarragon.
SERVES 4-6

CHICKEN, ASPARAGUS AND TARRAGON

This delicious, delicate soup is a simple way to bring out the best in asparagus, which grows better in the sandy soils of Eastern England than in any other part of the world.

500g/1lb asparagus
50g/2oz butter
125g/4oz celery, sliced
125g/4oz leeks, sliced
125g/4oz onions, sliced
Salt and white pepper
50g/2oz plain flour
1.25 litres/2 pints Chicken Stock (see page 147)
300g/10oz cooked chicken, cut into cubes
1 tsp chopped fresh thyme
2 bay leaves
200ml/7fl oz double cream
2 tbs chopped fresh tarragon

• Trim the bottom of the asparagus stalks where they start to turn white, then cut each stalk in half. Roughly chop the thick end, then slice the spear end into 3cm/1½ inch sections, keeping the two separate.
• Melt the butter in a pan, add the celery, leek and onion and fry gently until soft, seasoning with a little salt and white pepper. Mix in the flour with a wooden spoon. Heat up the stock in a separate pan, and whisk it into the vegetable mixture over medium heat. As soon as it comes to the boil, throw in the roughly chopped asparagus and simmer for 5 minutes. Then blend the mixture in a food processor.
• Now slip in the remaining asparagus, the chicken pieces, thyme and bay leaves. Simmer for 10 minutes, then pour in the cream, sprinkle the chopped tarragon on top, and serve.
SERVES 4-6

DUTCH PEA AND PORK

The Dutch have a bit of a thing for pea soups. Some excellent versions are made with beef, others, such as the one that follows, with ham. Traditionally, the ham would be boiled with the split peas, but in our version it becomes a garnish, in the form of succulent strips of crispy pork belly.

400g/13oz pork belly, cut into strips
½ tsp caraway seeds
½ tsp paprika
Salt and freshly ground black pepper
50g/2oz green split peas, soaked overnight, then drained
2 litres/3½ pints rich Beef Stock (see page 148)
50g/2oz butter
300g/10oz leeks, sliced
200g/7oz onions, sliced
425g/14oz potatoes, peeled and roughly chopped
125ml/4fl oz red wine
1 tbs chopped dill, to garnish

• Coat the pork belly in the paprika, salt and black pepper, and bake, skin side up in a hot oven, (220°C/425°F/gas 7) for 35 minutes or until the skin is nice and brown and crisped up.
• Place the split peas and stock in a large pan and simmer for 1½ hours. During the last 10 minutes, melt the butter in a pan, add the caraway seeds, leeks and onions and sweat gently until soft. Add this mixture to the peas along with the potatoes. Add the red wine (and extra stock or water if the mixture is too thick), and simmer for 30 minutes. The soup should now have a mushy texture.
• Blend half the soup in a food processor, return it to the pan and adjust the seasoning.
• Serve the soup garnished with the pork belly strips and the chopped dill.
SERVES 4-6 [G]

MUSSEL AND SAFFRON

1kg/2lb mussels
50g/2oz butter
125g/4oz carrot, sliced
125g/4oz celery, sliced
150g/5oz onion, chopped
1 tsp chopped garlic
200g/7oz frozen mussel
   meat, defrosted
Pinch of saffron
200ml/7fl oz white wine
50g/2oz plain white flour
900ml/1½ pints Fish Stock
   (see page 149)
1 large red pepper, roasted,
   skinned, cored and
   deseeded
1 tsp orange zest
2 bay leaves
1 sprig of thyme
200ml/7fl oz double cream
2 tsp chopped flat-leaf
   parsley

It isn't a combination that nature would necessarily have suggested, but this marriage of hardy molluscs and flimsy crocus stamens is definitely one made in heaven. By weight, saffron is the most expensive spice in the world at around £1000 a kilo/2lb, but don't panic, a little goes a very long way. Mussels aren't called what they are for nothing, being essentially solid muscle, which comes in handy if you spend your life clinging to wave-battered rocks. The frozen ones are a bit of a departure from our usual philosophy, but they do add body and save a lot of extra shelling.

• Scrub the mussels carefully, scraping off any barnacles and pulling out any stray seaweed still attached to the shell. Then steep in a bucket of water with a little flour sprinkled in it for a couple of hours to cleanse the mussels of sand. Finally, go through them one by one, making sure the shells are tightly closed, otherwise discard them.
• Melt the butter in a large pan, add the carrot, celery, onion and garlic and fry gently until soft. Then add the mussels in their shells, clamp the lid on tightly, turn up the heat for a couple of minutes, then turn it back down to low and cook for 8 minutes. Remove the lid. All the mussels should now be open and have released their juices into the pan. Allow them to cool and remove most of the mussels from the shells, leaving a few in their shells for a garnish.
• Return the shelled mussels to the pan with the defrosted ones, add the saffron and white wine, and reduce for a few minutes. Meanwhile, heat up the fish stock in another pan. Stir the flour into the mussels, then add the hot fish stock, roasted pepper and orange zest, and mix until smooth. Add the bay leaves and thyme, simmer for another 10 minutes, then remove the herbs. Add the cream, bring to the boil and serve garnished with the reserved mussels in their shells and the parsley.
SERVES 4-6

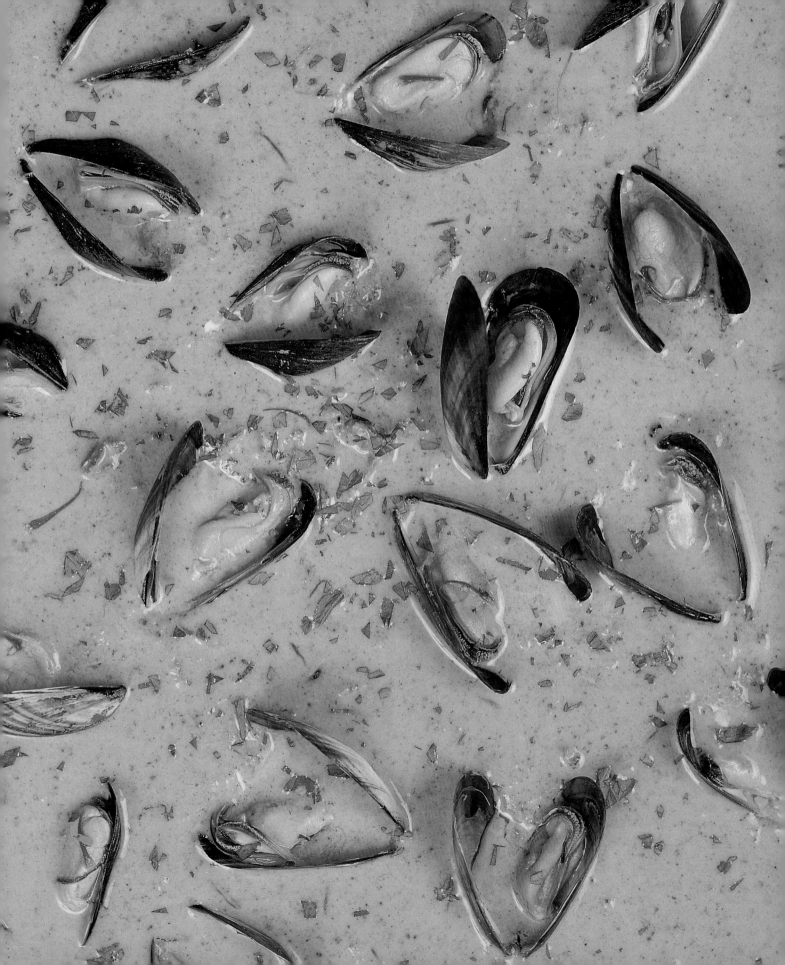

CALDO GALLEGO

This thick stew hails from Galicia in the north–west of Spain, where it warms the cockles of the heart when fierce Atlantic storms lash the region in winter. The actual contents are likely to vary according to the chef's whim and larder contents, but the three constants are chorizo (spicy pork and pimento sausages), tomatoes and chickpeas. Caldo Gallego is rich and moreish, and simply demands to be made in large quantities.

500g/1lb dried chickpeas, soaked overnight
425g/14oz belly pork
8 tomatoes, roasted, skinned and deseeded
2 red peppers, roasted, skinned, cored and deseeded
Paprika
425g/14oz chorizo, sliced thinly and slightly on the diagonal.
300g/10oz onions, chopped
4 cloves garlic, chopped
2 litres/3½ pints Beef Stock (see page 148)
2 medium potatoes, cut into 1cm/½ in cubes
4 cloves
4 bay leaves
2 sprigs of thyme
Salt and freshly ground black pepper
1 small bunch flat-leaf parsley

• Drain the chickpeas and place in a pan with water to cover. Boil until soft, 1–1½ hours; reserve.
• Preheat the oven to 230°C/ 450°F/ gas 8. Place the belly pork in a roasting tin, season with salt, pepper and paprika. Roast skin-side up until the skin has crisped, about 30 minutes. Roast the red peppers and tomatoes in a separate tin for 30 minutes at the same temperature. Chop the pork into 2.5cm/1in chunks, reserve the fat.
• Prepare the peppers and skin the tomatoes. Blend in a food processor with a little of the stock and reserve.
• Heat the belly pork fat in a large pan and fry the chorizo until lightly browned. Remove with a slotted spoon and reserve. Add the onion and garlic, fry gently until soft, then add the red pepper and tomato purée and cook for 2–3 minutes. Heat the stock, then add it to the pan with the chorizo, chickpeas, potatoes, cloves, bay leaves and thyme. Season to taste and simmer for 30 minutes. Serve sprinkled with the pork and parsley.
SERVES 8 -10 [G][D]

LAMB CAWL

This warming and satisfying stew is just the thing for St David's Day (March 1st). Cawl is simply the Welsh for stew, and this one celebrates the two ingredients most associated with that country – sheep and leeks. Mutton, if you can get hold of it (try a halal butcher), is more flavoursome than lamb and comfortingly old-fashioned. Like so many stews, this one gets better with age.

50g/2oz butter
150g/5oz carrot, diced
200g/7oz onion, sliced
400g/13oz leek, sliced
1 large parsnip, diced
600g/1¼lb lamb or mutton fillet, cut into 2.5cm/1in chunks
1.5 litres/2½ pints Lamb Stock (see page 149)
600g/1¼lb new potatoes, diced
4 bay leaves
1 sprig of thyme
1 swede, diced
Salt and black pepper to taste
1 tbs chopped flat-leaf parsley, to garnish

• Melt the butter in a large pan, then add the carrot, onion, leek and parsnip. Cover and sweat gently with the lamb for 10 minutes or so. Meanwhile, heat up the stock in a separate pan. Add the stock to the lamb with the potatoes, bay leaves, thyme, swede and a little salt and pepper. Simmer over gentle heat for about 2 hours, after which time the cawl will melt in your mouth. Serve garnished with a little parsley.
SERVES 6 [G]

BUBBLE AND SQUEAK SOUP

Nick frequents a small but popular café near the River Kennet, where he fishes. Every morning, an unshapely mound of vegetables is piled on the griddle, steaming and sizzling. One time, he asked the waitress what it was. "It's Squeak, love" she squawked. "Where's the Bubble?" our chef demanded. The waitress looked confused, then announced "the Bubble's in trouble." Nick is still trying to work out what she meant but he has breakfasted on Squeak ever since. B & S is typically comprised of vegetable leftovers and is a great dish for a chilly winter's day. Here is Nick's groundbreaking Bubble & Squeak soup recipe.

150g/5oz thinly sliced streaky bacon
1 medium diced carrot, approx. 100g
1 medium onion, approx. 100g
3 sticks of celery, sliced, approx. 100g
½ a leek, sliced
1 heaped tbs butter, approx. 30g
100g thinly sliced streaky bacon cut into small squares
400g/13oz potato, thinly sliced, then simmered in 1.2 litres of chicken stock for 20 mins or until soft
Half a small Savoy cabbage, shredded
100ml double cream
Salt
Freshly ground black pepper
A sprig of flat leaf parsley and sage

• Grill the thinly sliced streaky bacon until crispy. Reserve.
• Gently fry the carrot, leek, celery, onion and diced streaky bacon in the butter for about 15 minutes until soft.
• Blend the potatoes with the chicken stock until smooth, then pour in with the vegetables. Add the Savoy cabbage and simmer on for ten minutes.
• Add the double cream, then season with the salt and pepper.
• Garnish with parsley, sage and the crispy bacon.
SERVES 4 [G]

FAT-FREE MUSHROOM SOUP

Mushrooms, as you may or not know, are our other big thing in life. You can read all about our fungal adventures in Mushroom, published by Kyle Cathie. But the key point for now is that they make for some terrific soups. Unfortunately for the figure conscious, these are nearly always creamy, buttery, fatty affairs. Such was the thinking behind this delicious but low-cal recipe. Eat as much of it as you like. Try replacing the field mushrooms with varieties such as shiitake or fresh porcini, and if you decide to pull out of your diet at the last moment, finish it off with a dollop of crème fraiche.

100g/3½oz celery, sliced
100g/3½oz carrot, sliced
100g/3½oz onion, sliced
1200ml/2 pints water
3 cloves garlic, chopped
400g/13oz field mushrooms, sliced
300g/10oz potato, roughly chopped
25g dried porcini
1 tsp chopped ginger
2 tbs soy sauce
1 tsp chopped garlic
1 tsp of cep or shiitake mushroom essence, available from large supermarkets or speciality stockists, but not essential
salt and cracked black pepper to taste

• Simmer all the ingredients together for at least 45 minutes until soft and slushy.
• Blend in a food processor until smooth.
• Serve garnished with a few leaves of flat leaf parsley.
SERVES 4 [V] [L] [D] [G]

ELDERBERRY WITH SEMOLINA DUMPLINGS

THE SOUP

10 bunches ripe
    elderberries, stalks
    removed

200ml/7fl oz apple juice

400ml/14fl oz water

4 tbs clear honey

Juice of 1 lemon

1 cinnamon stick

4 drops vanilla essence

2 tbs cornflour

200ml/7fl oz crème fraîche

THE DUMPLINGS

75ml/3fl oz milk

75ml/3fl oz double cream

2 drops vanilla essence

1 cinnamon stick

1 tbs clear honey

75ml/3fl oz semolina
    (by volume)

Elderberries, which grow in black, shiny clusters, are not commonly available in the shops, but you can always go out and pick them – they ripen in the late summer/early autumn. They have a delicate, slightly musty flavour that combines particularly well with apple juice in the following sweet, Germanic dessert soup. Elderberries also have medicinal properties. This was discovered during 18th-century sea voyages, when somebody noticed that the people who drank cheap port adulterated with elderberries were warding off diseases far more effectively than their colleagues drinking the real McCoy.

• Place the elderberries in a pan with the apple juice, water, honey, lemon juice, cinnamon and vanilla. Simmer for 30 minutes, then push the mixture through a fine sieve into a bowl.

• Combine the cornflour with the crème fraîche and thoroughly mix this with a cup of the elderberry liquid. Place the remaining elderberry liquid in a pan over gentle heat. Pour the cornflour mixture into the soup and whisk it in. Slowly simmer until the soup thickens slightly. Remove from the heat, cover and allow to cool, then refrigerate.

• To make the dumplings, heat the milk and cream in a pan with the vanilla, cinnamon stick and honey. Simmer for 5 minutes, then remove the cinnamon and whisk in the semolina. It cooks very quickly, so whisk continuously to avoid lumps. After a few minutes the semolina mixture will have the consistency of thick mashed potato. Remove from the heat and allow to cool a little, then roll into little balls to be served in the chilled soup.

MAKES 4-6 SMALL PORTIONS [v]

JERUSALEM ARTICHOKE WITH CHIPS

Jerusalem artichokes have very little to do with Israel, the name deriving from the Italian *girosol*, meaning sunflower. Among the most tasty of all vegetables, they do have one slight drawback. Modesty dictates that we leave it to one John Goodyear, among the first to grow it in Europe, to describe: 'They stir up and cause a filthie loathsome stinking winde within the bodie'. Thank you John. Don't let this put you off, but choose your dinner companions carefully. The artichoke chips are a master stroke, providing a great texture contrast to the smooth, creamy soup.

THE CHIPS
200g/7oz Jerusalem
 artichokes, peeled
Vegetable oil, for
 frying
20-30 fresh sage leaves
Salt
THE SOUP
75g/3oz butter
50g/2oz carrot, chopped
50g/2oz leek, chopped
50g/2oz celery,
 chopped
125g/4oz onion,
 chopped
600g/1¼lb Jerusalem
 artichokes, peeled
 and sliced
1.25 litres/2 pints
 Chicken or Vegetable
 Stock (see pages
 147)
150ml/¼ pint double
 cream
Salt and white pepper
1 tbs chopped parsley

• To make the chips, slice the artichokes thinly with a mandolin. Heat about 1cm/½in of vegetable oil in a frying pan to 180–190°C/350–375°F. Gently lay the slices of artichoke in it, and fry until golden brown. Remove with a slotted spoon, drain on kitchen paper and sprinkle with salt. Do likewise with the sage leaves.
• Begin the soup by melting the butter in a large pan. Add the carrot, leek, celery, onion and artichokes, cover and leave to sweat over gentle heat for 10 minutes or so, stirring occasionally to prevent them sticking. Heat the stock in a separate pan. Now pour in the heated stock, and simmer until the vegetables are well softened. Blend in a food processor. Return to the pan and stir in the double cream. Season to taste, and garnish with chopped parsley. Serve with a heap of the artichoke and sage chips on each portion.
SERVES 4-6 [OPTIONALLY V] [G]

BRITISH COASTAL FISH STEW

This creamy stew is served with grated Cheddar and sage croûtons; it is good enough to give any of its Mediterranean cousins a good run for their money. Good quality fish is essential.

THE CROUTONS
10 fresh sage leaves
A few slices of stale
 bread, cut into
 2.5cm/1in chunks
1 tbs olive oil
Salt and freshly ground
 black pepper
THE STEW
50g/2oz butter
125g/4oz carrot, cut
 into 1cm/½in cubes
125g/4oz leek, sliced
125g/4oz onion, sliced
125g/4oz celery, sliced
1.25 litres/2 pints Fish
 Stock (see page 149)
50g/2oz plain flour
300g/10oz new potatoes,
 cut into 1-2.5cm/½-1
 in cubes and boiled
 for 10 minutes
200g/7oz little cooked
 prawns, shelled
200g/7oz cod fillet, cut
 into 2.5cm/1in chunks
200g/7oz haddock
 fillet, cut into
 2.5cm/1in chunks
150ml/¼ pint double
 cream
Salt and white pepper
150g/5oz mature
 Cheddar, grated, to
 garnish

• Preheat the oven to 200°C/400°F/gas 6. To make the croûtons, chop up the sage leaves and toss them with the bread cubes in olive oil, salt and pepper. Spread on a baking sheet and bake for 15 minutes. Remove and allow to cool.
• Melt the butter in a large pan, add the carrots, leek, onion and celery, cover and cook gently for 5–10 minutes until soft. Meanwhile, heat up the stock in a separate pan. Mix the flour into the vegetables until it is well incorporated. Slowly whisk the stock into the mixture, and bring to the boil. Now add the prawns, fish, cream and the cooked potatoes. Season to taste and simmer for a few more minutes, stirring a little.
• Serve garnished with the croûtons and the grated Cheddar.
SERVES 4-6

ARTICHOKE WITH SALMON AND SORREL

Globe rather than Jerusalem artichokes are the operative vegetables in this superlative soup, a relief to anyone unlucky enough to have found themselves inflating suspiciously upon sampling our delicious Jerusalem Artichoke Soup with Chips (see page 22). Salmon use to swim up the Thames in their millions to mate, while the sorrel growing in the rough pastures of the upper reaches of the river could only look on at the orgies which developed. In this soup, the two are married at last, the slightly bitter sorrel combining with the sweetness of the salmon to mutual benefit.

The hearts of 4 large cooked globe artichokes
50g/2oz butter
125g/4oz carrots, sliced
125g/4oz leeks, sliced
125g/4oz celery, sliced
1.25 litres/2 pints Fish Stock (see page 149)
50g/2oz plain flour
500g/1lb salmon fillets, cut into 2.5cm/1in chunks
150ml/¼ pint double cream
1 tbs chopped tarragon
1 tbs chopped parsley
Salt and white pepper
50g/2oz sorrel leaves, shredded

• Chop the hearts and set aside.
• Melt the butter in a large pan. Add the carrot, leek and celery, cover and sweat gently until soft, then mix in the flour and cook for 2 minutes. Heat the stock in a pan.
• Add the stock to the vegetables and bring to the boil briefly. Add the artichoke hearts and half the salmon; blend in a food processor.
• Return to the pan and add the remaining salmon, the cream and the herbs. Season to taste, and bring to the boil for a second. Add the sorrel just before serving, as it loses its flavour extremely fast in the hot soup.

SERVES 4-6

SMOKED HADDOCK AND LEEK CHOWDER

Neither knew it, but the leek and the haddock were made for each other. This is a traditional English version of Scottish Cullen Skink, and is best made with undyed smoked haddock.

500g/1lb smoked haddock
50g/2oz butter
400g/13oz leeks, chopped
125g/4oz onion, chopped
1.25 litres/2 pints Fish Stock (see page 149)
300g/10oz cooked, mashed potato
200ml/7fl oz double cream
Salt and black pepper
1 tbs chopped parsley

• Either get the fishmonger to skin the fish or, if you feel confident, do it yourself. This involves inserting a filleting knife between the skin and the flesh at the tail end and grabbing hold of the raised skin between the thumb and forefinger of your other hand. You then cut along the fish, keeping the knife horizontal to the work surface, as you pull the skin towards you. Either way, cut the haddock into 1-2.5cm(½-1in) chunks.
• Melt the butter in a large pan and add the leek and onion. Cover and sweat over gentle heat until they soften. Meanwhile, heat up the stock. Stir the potato into the vegetables, then the stock, and stir in the haddock. Simmer for 5 minutes, add the cream and chopped parsley and serve.

SERVES 4-6 [G]

Mediter-
ranean

ITALY, SPAIN and the South of France each have distinctive cuisines, and considerable regional variations within their own boundaries into the bargain. Yet take a soup from any of these countries, serve it to somebody blindfolded, and there is an excellent chance that they will know at once what part of the world it comes from. The signature notes of olive oil, aromatic herbs and the best tomatoes in the world are simply unmistakable.

The story begins with the olive tree. Some time between five and six thousand years ago, the residents of the Eastern Mediterranean discovered that with careful pruning and judicious position-ing, the scrubby indigenous olive bush could provide a virtually inexhaustible source of fragrant, nourishing oil. The Ancient Greeks, seeing the commercial opportunity, felled entire forests to found an export industry based on this magical new foodstuff. By Roman times, connoisseur-ship of olive oil had reached levels to match that of the wine buffs of the present. Healthy, pure and delicious, the olive has kept the Mediterranean in its grip ever since.

In addition to their prominence in the Ancient World, Italy, Spain and France were at the centre of the revolution brought about by the discovery of the New World at the end of the fifteenth century. They were therefore the first Europeans to get their hands on the second great ingredient of Mediterranean soup-making – the tomato. Nevertheless, it took a fair while for the potential of this strange fruit-come-vegetable to be realised. The first tomatoes to arrive in Europe were unpromisingly yellow (hence the Italian name *pomodoro*, or golden apple). The people of Provence preferred to call them 'love apples', and were more inclined to grow them as ornamental shrubs than actually risk eating them. But in the Eighteenth Century, Italian Jesuits returned home with rather more appetising red varieties, and the Mediterranean love affair with the tomato extended to the stomach.

The third great defining element in Mediterranean soup-making, aromatic herbs, had been growing wild and perfuming the air of the region's hillsides long before there was any soup to be made. Some – particularly bay and basil – were important enough to the Greeks and Romans to attain great religious significance, as well as respect for their therapeutic properties. Eating a herb-infused soup in the Mediterranean is not only good for you; it is a little like consuming the best of the air.

There is of course, much more to soup in the Mediterranean than olive oil, tomatoes and herbs – garlic and seafood deserve a mention, for a start. But these ingredients have had a crucial role in the development of some of the best known and justifiably well-loved soups and stews in the world.

COLD COURGETTE AND MINT WITH GRAIN MUSTARD

This is simple, creamy, tangy and very, very refreshing. We use chicken stock for a fuller flavour, but there is no reason for vegetarians to deprive themselves the pleasure.

600g/1¼lb courgettes
Salt and freshly ground black pepper
Olive oil
200ml/7fl oz double cream
1 heaped tbs grain mustard
1 tbs lemon juice
1 litre/1¾ pints Chicken or Vegetable Stock (see page 147)
2 tbs balsamic vinegar
½ cucumber
2 cloves garlic
125g/4oz onion, chopped
1 bunch of mint

• Preheat the oven to 200°C/400°F/gas 6. Trim the courgettes, season with salt and black pepper and brush with olive oil. Bake for 30 minutes, then allow to cool. Cut into chunks.
• Blend all the ingredients together in a food processor, leaving a few mint leaves to garnish. Chill for a few hours before serving.
SERVES 4-6 [OPTIONALLY V][G]

SPANISH SEAFOOD STEW

When we served this in SOUP works it invariably sold out, despite being one of our most expensive offerings. With its blend of piquancy and meltingly tender fish, this is a stew to rival the great bouillabaise. We like to leave the clusters of squid tentacles intact, so they look like tiny Medusas adrift in a delicious red sea.

250g/8oz onion
2 tbs olive oil
125g/4oz celery, sliced
125g/4oz leek, sliced
1 tsp chopped garlic
1 tsp paprika
½ tsp chilli powder
1 litre/1¾ pints Fish Stock (see page 149)
50g/2oz plain flour
300ml/½ pint passata
3 large red peppers, roasted, skinned, cored and deseeded
1 aubergine, roasted and cut into chunks
2 bay leaves
1 sprig of thyme
250g/8oz cod fillet, cut into chunks
250g/8oz baby squid, sliced into rings, tentacles left whole
250g/8oz raw prawns
1 tbs lemon juice
1 tbs chopped oregano, plus whole leaves to garnish
1 tbs chopped flat-leaf parsley
Salt and freshly ground black pepper

• Roast the peppers and the aubergine in the following manner: slice in half lengthways, drizzle with olive oil, season and bake at 200°C/400°F/gas 6 for 35 minutes.
• Chop the onion roughly. Heat the oil in a large pan, add the celery, leek, onion, garlic, paprika and chilli powder, and fry gently until the vegetables are nicely softened. Meanwhile, heat up the stock in a separate pan. Stir in the flour until it is completely incorporated, add the passata, then gradually add the fish stock, whisking constantly.
• Chop the peppers into small pieces and add to the pan with the aubergine, bay leaves and thyme. Simmer for 20 minutes, stirring occasionally. Add the remaining ingredients and simmer for just 3-5 minutes longer, ensuring that the herbs keep their colour and the fish does not become overcooked. Garnish with the parsley. Serve and be glad.
SERVES 4-6 [L][D]

MEDITERRANEAN TOMATO SOUP

Only make this if you have a pile of ripe, flavoursome tomatoes. We recently made a batch using cherry tomatoes which had ripened on the vine. The flavour was sweet and intense.

1 kg/2lb fresh ripe
 tomatoes
2 tbs olive oil
4 medium shallots
 peeled and roughly
 chopped
250g/8oz diced potato
1 level tbs roasted
 garlic purée (see
 page 157)
1 tbs tomato purée
 (see page 157)
1 tbs sun-dried tomato
 paste
500ml/17fl oz Chicken
 or Vegetable Stock
 (see page 147)
Salt and freshly
 ground black pepper
1 bunch basil

• Preheat the oven to 200°C/ 400°F/gas 6.
• Roughly chop the tomatoes and roast in a baking dish with the olive oil and the shallots for 40 minutes until slightly browned. Meanwhile, simmer the potato for 20 minutes or until soft and reserve.
• Empty the roasted tomato mixture into a large pan along with the potatoes, stock, roasted garlic, tomato purée and sun-dried tomato paste.
• Simmer for 30 minutes, topping up with stock or water if necessary.
• Blend until smooth.
• Season with salt and pepper and garnish with lots of fresh basil.
• This soup can be eaten hot or cold.
SERVES 4 [D][V][L]

MARMITAKO

This terrific soup is named after the *marmita*, or large earthenware pot, in which it is traditionally prepared by Europe's oldest inhabitants, the Basques.

4 red peppers, roasted,
 skinned, deseeded,
 cored and chopped
50ml/2fl oz olive oil
200g/7oz onion,
 chopped
4 cloves garlic,
 chopped
½ tsp cayenne pepper
1½ tsp paprika
10 tomatoes, peeled
 and chopped
1 litre/1¾ pints Fish
 Stock (see page
 149)
200ml/7fl oz white
 wine
800g/1lb 10oz
 potatoes, peeled and
 cut into small
 chunks
800g/1lb 10oz fresh
 tuna fillet, cut into
 chunks
1 small bunch flat-leaf
 parsley, chopped
1 small bunch oregano,
 chopped
1 small bunch basil,
 chopped
1 sprig of thyme
Salt and freshly
 ground black pepper
Juice of 1 lemon

• Preheat the oven to 230°C/450°F/gas 8. Place the peppers on a baking sheet and roast for about 30 minutes. Remove, place in a plastic bag and seal. When cool, skin, deseed, chop and reserve.
• Heat the olive oil in a large pan. Add the onion, garlic, cayenne and paprika and fry over moderate heat until soft, then add the tomatoes and continue cooking until the tomatoes have become mushy.
• Pour in the stock and white wine, add the potatoes and simmer for 30 minutes. Add the tuna, herbs, peppers and seasoning to taste and simmer for a further 10 minutes.
• Leave the marmitako to rest for a couple of minutes, then serve with the lemon juice sprinkled on top.
SERVES 6 [D][G][L]

ROAST AUBERGINE AND RED PEPPER

This soup pretty much sums up the Mediterranean, and gives the lie to the myth that vegetarian foods lack flavour. It is made with cool summer evenings in mind.

**2 medium aubergines,
    about 600g/1¼lb**
**Salt and freshly ground
    black pepper**
150ml/¼ pint olive oil
1 head of garlic
4 large red peppers
125g/4oz celery, sliced
200g/7oz onion, sliced
**1 litre/1¾ pints Vegetable
    Stock (see page 147)**
50g/2oz plain flour
600ml/1 pint passata
2 tbs chopped basil
2 tbs chopped oregano
2 tbs chopped parsley
2 bay leaves
1 sprig of thyme

• Preheat the oven to 240°C/475°F/gas 9. Cut the aubergines down the middle, and place the halves face up on a baking tray. Sprinkle with salt and pepper, drizzle with olive oil, and roast for 20 minutes in the oven with the peppers and the whole head of garlic, unpeeled, alongside. As soon as you take the peppers out of the oven, place them in a plastic bag, seal and leave to cool. Peel and core the peppers, then cut them into strips. Cut the aubergine into small chunks and squeeze out the softened garlic.

• Heat the remaining oil in a large pan over medium heat. Add the celery and onion, cover and sweat until soft. Meanwhile, heat up the stock in a separate pan. Stir the flour, passata and garlic into the vegetables, then gradually whisk in the stock. Bring to the boil, reduce to a simmer, and add the remaining ingredients, stirring continuously. Adjust the seasoning, remove the bay leaves and serve immediately.

SERVES 4-6 [V][L][D]

AJO BLANCO

200g/7oz ground almonds
3 cloves garlic
2 tbs olive oil
1 tbs white wine vinegar
125g/4oz white bread,
    crusts removed
750ml/1¼ pints water
200ml/7fl oz grape juice
125ml/4fl oz double cream
500g/1lb green grapes,
    peeled, halved and
    deseeded
Salt
2 tbs toasted almond flakes

This luxurious, creamy soup may sound a little strange, but believe us, it works. Essentially a kind of white gazpacho, it will transport you in a jiffy to the sun-drenched coast of Andalusia. Removing the seeds from the grapes is a minor hassle, but in our view a worthwhile one given the superior flavour of seeded grapes over their seedless cousins. Anyway, this is a soup you don't even have to cook!

• Process the almonds, garlic, oil and vinegar in a food processor, then slowly add the bread, water and grape juice until you have a medium consistency paste.
• Pour the mixture into a serving bowl, stir in the cream and the grapes, then chill. Add salt to taste. Serve sprinkled with the toasted almonds at the last minute.
SERVES 4-6 [v]

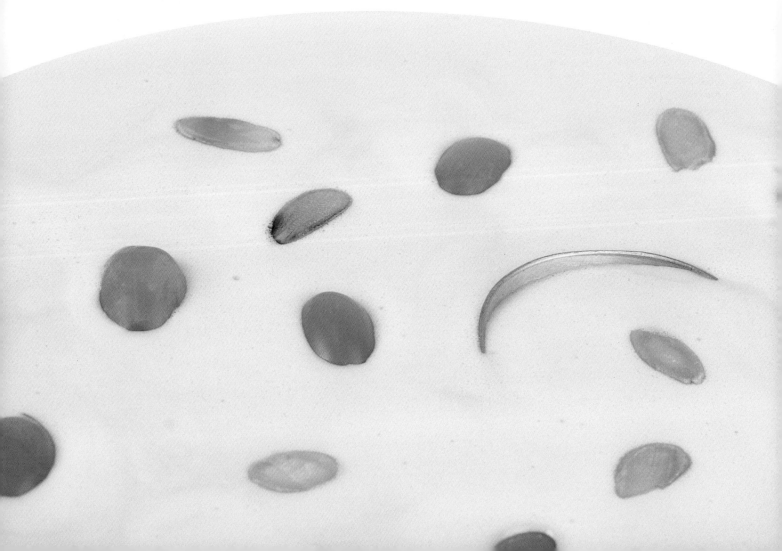

CATAPLANA

OK, Portugal isn't strictly speaking a Mediterranean country, but we felt that this spicy stew belongs in this section spiritually if not geographically. A comparison with the superficially rather similar Caldo Gallego in the Western Europe chapter (see page 18) should show you why: southern exotica such as olive oil, passata, chillies and coriander are starting to creep into the picture, and that is Mediterranean enough for us. Anyhow, it is delicious, rich and satisfying, so if the Portuguese don't mind, we'll just get on with the recipe.

• Preheat the oven to 230°C/450°F/gas 8. Place the chorizo and belly pork in a roasting tin and roast for about 20 minutes, until they are slightly browned and have released a fair amount of fat. Remove from the tin and reserve. Roast the tomatoes in a separate tin at the same time. Add them to the passata and blend in a food processor, then reserve.
• Heat the oil in a large pan, add the onions and garlic, cover and sweat over a moderate heat with the chorizo, pork, peppers, chillies, paprika, cumin, cinnamon, nutmeg and allspice. Stir the mixture constantly. Meanwhle, heat up the stock in a separate pan.
• Stir in the flour until it is completely incorporated, then gradually whisk in the stock and the tomato mixture. Bring to the boil, then reduce to a simmer for a few minutes, and season. Add the thyme and bay leaves and simmer for a further 10 minutes. Throw in the prawns or clams, simmer for 2–3 more minutes, and serve garnished with coriander.

SERVES 6-8 [D]

200g/7oz chorizo, cut into chunks
200g/7oz belly pork, cut into chunks
8 medium tomatoes
150ml/¼ pint passata
25ml/1fl oz olive oil
250g/8oz onion, chopped
4 cloves garlic, chopped
2 red peppers, chopped, cored and deseeded
2 red chillies, chopped and deseeded
1 tsp paprika
1 tsp cumin seed
¼ tsp ground cinnamon
¼ tsp ground nutmeg
¼ tsp ground allspice
1.25 litres/2 pints Chicken Stock (see page 147)
50g/2oz plain flour
Salt and freshly ground black pepper
2 bay leaves
1 sprig of thyme
200g/7oz raw prawns, shelled, or clams if available (for greater authenticity)
1 small bunch coriander, chopped, to garnish.

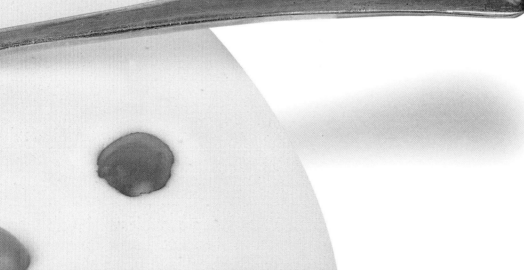

BEEF BOURGUIGNON

This venerable French stew is one of the most time-consuming items in this book, but it is good enough to make it all seem worthwhile. Beef Bourguignon is celebratory, dinner party fare, and will put feathers on your chest in the depths of winter.

300g/10oz shallots, peeled
1 tbs balsamic vinegar
1 tbs brown sugar
2 litres/3½ pints Beef
    Stock (see page 148)
½ bottle red wine
125g/4oz carrot, sliced
125g/4oz leek, sliced
125g/4oz celery, sliced
125g/4oz onion, sliced
50g/2oz butter
50g/2oz plain flour
1 tbs tomato purée
1 tbs olive oil
425g/14oz lean beef, cut
    into 2.5cm/1in cubes
250g/8oz baby button
    mushrooms, stalks cut
    off
2 bunches baby carrots,
    whole, with a little
    greenery left on top
sprig of thyme
4 bay leaves
Salt and freshly ground
    black pepper

• Preheat the oven to 220°C/425°F/gas 7. Place the shallots in a roasting tin, sprinkle with the balsamic vinegar and brown sugar and bake for 20 minutes to caramelise them.
• Place the stock and wine in a pan and simmer over moderate heat until reduced by half.
• Melt the butter in a large pan, add the carrot, leek, celery and onion, cover and sweat over gentle heat for 10 minutes. Stir in the flour, add the tomato purée, and pour in the hot stock, whisking vigorously to remove any lumps. Remove from the heat.
• Heat the olive oil in a frying pan and brown the meat on all sides, in batches if necessary. Remove the meat with a slotted spoon, reduce the heat and fry the mushrooms in the remaining oil (adding a little more if necessary) to give them a bit of colour.
• Return the stock and vegetable mixture to the heat, add the beef, mushrooms, shallots, bay leaves and thyme, cover and simmer for 1–1½ hours, stirring occasionally to prevent sticking. Adjust the seasoning and serve.
SERVES 6

TOULOUSE SAUSAGE AND BEAN CASSOULET

Recently, we supplied this stew for a friend's wedding in Paris. The caterers had a good old Gallic laugh when they heard they were going to be dishing up one of their regional specialities, cooked by an English chef. But when they tried it, their laughter was replaced by moans of ecstasy. This wonderfully porky stew is right at the top of our sales charts during the winter.

250g/8oz dried butter
    beans, soaked
    overnight
425g/14oz Toulouse
    sausage
50g/2oz duck and pork
    fat, left over from
    making the stock (see
    page 149)
150g/5oz onion, chopped
125/4oz carrot, cut into
    1cm/½ in cubes
125g/4oz celery, sliced
125g/4oz leek, sliced
150g/5oz unsmoked back
    bacon, chopped
1.25 litres/2 pints Duck
    and Pork Stock (see
    page 149)
50g/2oz plain flour
250ml/8fl oz passata
1 sprig of thyme
4 bay leaves
Salt and freshly ground
    black pepper.

• Drain the butter beans, place in a large pan with plenty of water and boil for 1–1½ hours until soft. Drain and reserve.
• Preheat the oven to 200°C/400°F/gas 6. Place the Toulouse sausage, which often comes in one continuous coil, in a roasting tin and cook for 15 minutes. Slice it into bite-sized chunks, and reserve, remembering to keep all the juices.
• Melt the fat in a large pan. Add the vegetables and bacon, cover and sweat over moderate heat for 10 minutes. Meanwhile, heat up the stock in a separate pan. Add the flour and turn the heat down. Stir the flour into the mixture until it has all been absorbed, turn up the heat again, and slowly whisk in the stock.
• Add the butter beans, sausage, passata and herbs to the pan. Bring to the boil, then reduce to a simmer for 10 minutes. Adjust the seasoning and serve.
SERVES 4-6

FISH SOUP WITH ROUILLE AND GRUYERE CROUTONS

THE CROUTONS
1 stale French loaf
150g/5oz Gruyère cheese,
 grated

THE ROUILLE
1 red pepper
2 red chillies, deseeded
3 cloves garlic
½ tsp ground cumin
½ tsp salt
A little freshly ground
 black pepper
125ml/4fl oz olive oil
1 slice of bread, soaked in
 water, then lightly
 squeezed
1 tbs lemon juice

THE SOUP
125ml/4fl oz olive oil
1 fennel bulb, sliced
4 cloves garlic, chopped
300g/10oz onion, sliced
1 tsp paprika
½ tsp chilli powder
200g/7oz carrots, sliced
200g/7oz leeks, sliced
1 tbs tomato purée
3 litres/5 pints Fish Stock
 (see page 149)
425g/14oz potato, peeled
 and cubed
2kg/4lb bouillabaisse mix
4 tomatoes, peeled,
 deseeded and chopped
Zest of 1 orange
1 large sprig of thyme
About 2 pinches of saffron
125ml/4fl oz white wine
4 bay leaves
Salt and white pepper

This puréed fish soup uses the marine creatures traditionally used in bouillabaisse, the quintessential Mediterranean speciality. The exact contents can vary considerably, essentially amounting to whatever is left in the fishing net after the more palatable-looking fish have been removed, but they always include rascasse, small crabs, lobsters and shrimps together with a few larger fish. Our supplier sells us a bouillabaisse mix, and you may find a quality fishmonger willing to do the same. Otherwise, you can gradually collect the requisite items and freeze them down, provided you gut them first.

To avert the wrath of Marseillaise purists, who are unbelievably strict about what they will and won't classify as a bouillabaisse, we've erred on the side of caution and just described this as fish soup. Whatever you want to call it, it is absolutely delicious, particularly with the rouille (an emulsification of olive oil and spices) and crisp Gruyère croûtons.

• Preheat the oven to 200°C/400°F/gas 6. To make croûtons, cut the bread into thin slices, sprinkle with Gruyère and bake for 5–10 minutes, watching like a hawk to ensure that they slightly brown but don't burn.
• Turn up the oven to 230°C/450°F/gas 8. To make the rouille, place the pepper on a baking sheet, sprinkle with oil and roast for 30 minutes. Remove and place in a plastic bag and seal. Skin and deseed when cool. Blend the pepper with all the other ingredients for the rouille in a food processor and the rouille is ready to go.
• To make the soup, heat the olive oil in a large pan. Add the fennel, garlic, onion, paprika, chilli powder, carrots and leeks and fry over a medium heat until soft, stirring frequently.
• Add the tomato purée and stir in, then pour in the stock and add the potatoes, bouillabaisse mix, tomatoes, orange zest, thyme, saffron, white wine and bay leaves. Simmer for an hour, then blend in batches in a food processor, making sure you first remove any pieces of fish bone or shell. Push the purée through a conical sieve to obtain every last drop of liquid. Return to the pan and reheat for 1–2 minutes.
• Serve with croûtons floating on the top, stir in the rouille and congratulate yourself.
SERVES 6-8

PROVENCAL CHICKEN WITH OLIVES

THE MARINADE

2 cloves garlic, chopped

1 tbs lemon juice

½ tsp paprika

Salt and freshly ground
black pepper

1 tbs olive oil

THE SOUP

1 medium aubergine

Salt and freshly ground
black pepper

425g/14oz chicken breasts

4 courgettes

4 red peppers

6 big tomatoes

1 head of garlic, top sliced
off

1 red onion, peeled and
halved

425ml/14fl oz passata or
tomato juice

125ml/4fl oz olive oil

125g/4oz white onion,
sliced

125g/4oz celery, sliced

1.25 litres/2 pints Chicken
Stock (see page 147)

1 small bunch oregano,
roughly chopped

1 small bunch basil,
roughly chopped

1 small bunch flat-leaf
parsley, roughly
chopped

1 sprig of thyme

2 bay leaves

250g/8oz pitted black
olives

The key to success with this luscious soup is browning the chicken sufficiently. Provençal olives are small and tasty and usually come with their stones still in. If you can find a pitted variety, it will save time.

• Slice the aubergine lengthwise, sprinkle with salt, and leave to stand for 20 minutes before wiping the salt off.

• Mix the marinade ingredients in a shallow dish and add the chicken. Turn to coat, then leave to marinate for 30 minutes.

• Preheat the oven to 230°C/450°F/gas 8. Place the aubergine, courgettes, peppers, tomatoes, garlic and onion in a large roasting tin, season with salt and black pepper and drizzle with olive oil, giving extra to the aubergine. Roast for 20 minutes, or until browned. Skin the tomatoes, add to the passata and blend in a food processor. Skin, core and deseed the red peppers. Roughly chop them with the other vegetables and reserve.

• Heat 2 tablespoons of olive oil in a frying pan over moderate heat. Remove the chicken from the marinade and fry for 5 minutes on each side until well browned. Allow to cool, and cut into 2.5cm/1in chunks.

• Heat the remaining olive oil in a large pan. Add the onion and celery and fry for about 5 minutes. Pour in the passata mixture and the stock. Bring to the boil, simmer for 2–3 minutes, and blend in a food processor.

• Return the soup to the pan, add the chopped vegetables and herbs, the olives and chicken, bring to the boil for a split second, season to taste and serve.

SERVES 4-6 [G][D]

Eastern Europe

HISTORY, geography and climate are key factors in determining the character of a region's soups and stews, but in Eastern Europe there seems to be more than the usual quota of all three!

On the history side, we are talking about a region that has been conquered and settled by a bewildering array of peoples: Magyars (paprika), Vikings (caraway seeds), Mongols (fermented milk products) and above all Slavs have all left their culinary stamp. The various religious traditions of Eastern Europe (Catholic, Orthodox, Jewish and Muslim) have also made important contributions to the mix. The Ashkenazi Jews, for instance, adapted local ingredients and traditions to the stringent demands of *kosher* cooking to produce some of the finest soups on the planet.

On the geographical front, Eastern Europe is every bit as diverse as might be expected of a region which stretches from the Arctic to the Black Sea and a great deal further West to East. But the unifying effect of the vast Russian Empire has allowed culinary cross-fertilization on a grand scale, marrying the typical flavours of the North (dill, caraway and poppy seeds) with those of the South (the fiery paprika and chillies of Hungary and Romania) to wondrous effect.

If there is one thing that has dominated the evolution of Eastern European soups above all else, however, it is the climate. The long, savage winters of the area have made the inhabitants masters of food-preserving techniques, giving the world such delights as *sauerkraut.* They have also made for ingenious ways with the few vegetables capable of being stored through the big freeze, notably beetroot, grains of various kinds, cabbages, and the potato. The resulting comfort soups, specifically designed to sustain farmers when it's 30 degrees below, are about as comforting as soups are going to get.

Eastern European summers, when they arrive, tend to be scorching. At this stage, the region's genius for cold soups thankfully kicks in. Chilled cucumber soup and borscht are refreshing staples. The Hungarians and Poles are particularly enamoured of fruit soups. Then as summer gives way to autumn, the Eastern Europeans' powerful foraging instincts (previously honed by the shortages associated with serfdom) come into full play. Even in the countryside surrounding London, your average mushroom hunter is as likely as not to be a Russian or Polish émigré. Wild fungi feature prominently in the recipes that follow.

Other recurrent notes in the soups and stews of Eastern Europe are dumplings, sour cream and delicious and sometimes eccentric tangs provided by pickles, capers, vinegar or lemon juice. One thing is certain: there is a whole lot more to Eastern European soup than borscht.

ICED CUCUMBER AND DILL

2 medium cucumbers
1 head of garlic
50ml/2fl oz light olive oil
1 tsp grain mustard
1 tbs lemon juice
150 ml/¼ pint double
    cream
A pinch or two of salt
300ml/½ pint Greek
    yoghurt
1 tbs white wine or
    balsamic vinegar
1 litre/1¾ pints Chicken
    Stock (see page 147)
125g/4oz white
    breadcrumbs
1 tbs chopped shallot
White pepper
2 tbs dill fronds

Cucumber is about the most refreshing of all vegetables, due to its extremely high water content. In some parts of Eastern Europe, children will even choose a cucumber over an ice-cream as a cooling summer snack. The one drawback is the unpredictable bitterness of some specimens. This can be pre-empted by salting them for 20 minutes (washing the salt off prior to use) or in the case of the smaller varieties, by peeling them. In any event, the problem rarely arises with the modern supermarket cucumber. We prefer to take the risk and leave half the skin on, because it colours the soup nicely.

• Peel one of the cucumbers, and de-seed both of them. Chop the one with the skin into 1cm/½in dice, and put aside. Roughly chop the other one.
• Preheat the oven to 220°C/425°F/gas 7. Wrap the garlic in foil with a drop or two of olive oil and roast in the oven for 25 minutes. Allow to cool, then squeeze out a couple of teaspoons of purée. You can keep the rest of the garlic in the fridge for up to a week to use in another dish.
• Place all the ingredients except the unpeeled cucumber and the dill in the food processor and blend until smooth. Refrigerate the mixture until chilled, and serve garnished with the cucumber cubes and dill.
SERVES 4-6

POLISH WILD MUSHROOM

Nick frequents a secret wood in West Sussex in his never-ending quest for wild fungi, but inevitably encounters an émigré Pole or two with fuller bags than his own. At least there is always the fall-back of dried porcini mushrooms, as used here...

50g/2oz dried porcini
   mushrooms
125ml/4fl oz warm
   water
75g/3oz butter
500g/1lb chestnut
   mushrooms
3 cloves garlic, chopped
125g/4oz carrot,
   chopped
125g/4oz leek,
   chopped
125g/4oz celery, sliced
125g/4oz onion, sliced
1.25 litres/2 pints
   Vegetable Stock
   (see page 147)
300g/10oz potatoes,
   peeled and sliced
Salt and freshly
   ground black pepper
2 tbs chopped dill
175ml/6fl oz sour cream

• Soak the porcini mushrooms in the warm water for half an hour. Strain through a fine sieve, reserving the liquid.
• Melt the butter in a large heavy pan. Add the mushrooms, garlic, carrot, leek, celery and onion, and fry until the mushrooms have reduced in size and released their liquor. Meanwhile, heat up the stock in a separate pan. Add the stock, potatoes, and the porcini and their liquid, and simmer for about 30 minutes, until the potatoes are soft. Blend the mixture in a food processor, leaving the soup fairly coarse in texture. Season to taste, and serve garnished with the dill and a dollop of sour cream.

SERVES 4-6 [V][G]

RUSSIAN FISH AND SPINACH STEW WITH SOUR CREAM

Russia is mind-bogglingly vast, stretching over ten time zones. Much of the country is about as far from the sea as it is possible to be, but where sea fish is available, the Russians certainly know what to do with it. The following soup is a case in point: this thick, wholesome stew is a meal in itself. The dill and sour cream give the soup its Eastern European feel.

1 litre/1¾ pints Fish
   Stock (see page 149)
½ bottle white wine
1 bouquet garni
50g/2oz butter
125g/4oz carrot,
   chopped
125g/4oz celery,
   chopped
125g/4oz leek, chopped
125g/4oz onion,
   chopped
50g/2oz plain flour
300g/10oz new potatoes
150g/5oz haddock fillet,
   cut into chunks
150g/5oz salmon fillet,
   cut into chunks
150g/5oz cod fillet, cut
   into chunks
300g/10oz spinach,
   washed and chopped
175g/6fl oz sour cream
1 tbs lemon juice
Zest of 1 lemon
Salt and white pepper
1 bunch chopped dill

• Heat the stock in a large pan with the wine and bouquet garni. Melt the butter in a heavy-bottomed pan, add the carrot, celery, leek and onion and fry slowly until softened. Stir in the flour until well incorporated, then gradually whisk in the hot stock, removing the bouquet garni. Meanwhile, dice and cook the new potatoes in salted, boiling water. Drain and add to the soup.
• Stir in the fish, spinach, 125ml/4fl oz of the sour cream, the lemon juice and lemon zest and season to taste. Bring to a rapid boil, making sure the fish does not overcook. Serve with a dollop of sour cream and a sprinkling of dill.

SERVES 6-8

CZECH CHICKEN AND CABBAGE SOUP WITH SAUERKRAUT

375g/12oz onion, sliced

375g/12oz celery, sliced

375g/12oz carrots, sliced

1 head of garlic

4 bay leaves

2 sprigs of thyme

50ml/2fl oz olive oil

3 litres/5 pints Chicken
   Stock (see page 147)

375g/12oz white cabbage,
   shredded

1 litre/1¾ pints passata

1 tbs paprika

1 tbs tabasco

2 tbs caraway seeds

Salt and freshly ground
   black pepper

500g/1lb chicken fillets,
   thinly sliced

500g/1lb sauerkraut

A handful of chopped flat-
   leaf parsley, reserving
   some for garnish

50g/2oz brown sugar

50ml/2fl oz lemon juice

For some reason, Nick finds himself unable to cook this soup in small quantities and the pans are inevitably overflowing once everything has been crammed in. But it is worth it. The tangy, salty sauerkraut combines with the juicy chicken to marvellous effect.

This wonderfully fortifying soup comes almost straight from the peasant stockpots of old, and demonstrates the typical Eastern European nous with preserved foods such as sauerkraut. And if anything will cure the common cold, this will.

• Preheat the oven to 190°C/375°F/gas 5. Place the onion, celery, carrot, garlic, bay leaves and thyme in a roasting tin with the olive oil, stir to coat well and then bake for half an hour.
• Heat the chicken stock in a very large pan and add the contents of the roasting tin together with the shredded cabbage, passata, paprika and seasonings. Simmer for half an hour, then skim off the fat and blot the surface with kitchen paper to absorb any remaining fat. Add the chicken, sauerkraut, most of the parsley, the sugar and lemon juice and simmer for 5 minutes. Serve steaming hot garnished with the remaining chopped parsley.
SERVES 10 [D][G]

BEETROOT BORSCHT WITH PIROZHKI AND FRESH PETRUSHKA

Not long ago, a tired-looking Russian woman dressed in tatters approached Nick, anxious to impart the recipes her mother had taught her. The following isn't actually one of them, but we thought we'd remember her anyway.

The soup below is a bit of a Tolstoyan epic, but definitely one to savour. *Pirozhki* are a kind of crescent-shaped Eastern ravioli, and they add bite and texture to this puréed version of borscht. *Petrushka* is simply the Russian word for flat-leaf parsley – we've left it untranslated to add a little oriental mystery. Poland, Lithuania and the Ukraine all have their individual takes on borscht, but this one is pure Nick. The base is a rich beef stock.

HUNGARIAN GOULASH WITH PUREED ROASTED PEPPERS

Hungarian cuisine is one of the world's unsung greats, and goulash (or *gulyasleves* as they call it in Budapest) is the nation's most famous dish. Every household has its own version, many incorporating ingredients such as cabbage, parsnip and carrot which do not appear in the recipe below but just as well might. The Magyars are the undisputed kings of paprika, which is particularly well complemented in this dish by the tangy roasted pepper purée.

THE SOUP
50g/2oz butter
125g/4oz carrot, sliced
175g/6oz onion, sliced
500g/1lb beetroot, peeled and chopped
4 cloves garlic, chopped
1.5 litres/2½ pints Beef Stock (see page 148)
25g/1oz plain flour
175ml/6fl oz passata
300g/10oz potatoes, peeled and sliced
3 tbs balsamic vinegar
Sugar, to taste
Salt and freshly ground black pepper
2 tbs chopped flat-leaf parsley
250ml/8fl oz sour cream

THE PIROZHKIS
25g/1oz butter
50g/2oz shallots, chopped
125g/4oz mixed courgette, carrot and mushroom, chopped
2 cloves garlic, chopped
1/2 tsp caraway seeds
1 tsp paprika
1 hard-boiled egg
250g/8oz cooked meat (chicken, beef or pork), finely chopped
1 tbs chopped flat-leaf parsley
Salt and freshly ground black pepper
300g/10oz shortcrust pastry
1 egg, beaten

• To make the soup, melt the butter in a large pan and gently fry the carrot, onion, beetroot and garlic for 15 minutes until the vegetables have softened a little. Meanwhile, heat up the beef stock in a separate pan, reserving 1 tablespoon for the pirozhkis. Stir in the flour, then gradually whisk in the hot beef stock, together with the passata. Add the potatoes and simmer for 40 minutes. Add the balsamic vinegar, and a little sugar and salt and pepper to taste. Blend thoroughly in a food processor until velvety smooth. Serve with chopped parsley and a blob of sour cream on each bowl.
• The pirozhkis can be served on the side and dunked into the borscht or added to the soup itself just before garnishing. Melt the butter in a frying pan, add the shallots and vegetables with the garlic, caraway seeds and paprika, and fry gently until soft. Chop and add the egg, meat and parsley, with salt and pepper to taste, and fry for 2–3 more minutes. Moisten with the reserved beef stock.
• Preheat the oven to 220°C/425°F/gas 7. Roll out the pastry, cut it into small rounds about 10cm/4in in diameter, and place a blob of the mixture on one side of each circle. Brush around the sides with the beaten egg, and fold over, crimping the edges. Brush the completed pirozhkis with the rest of the beaten egg and bake for 15–20 minutes.
SERVES 4-6

50g/2oz butter or preferably lard
750g/1½lb lean beef, cubed
300g/10oz chopped onion
3 cloves garlic, chopped
1 tsp caraway seeds
1–2 mildish red chillies, chopped and deseeded
1 level tbs paprika
50g/2oz plain flour
4 red peppers, roasted, skinned, cored, deseeded and puréed in a food processor
6 tomatoes, roasted, skinned and puréed in a food processor
1.25 litres/2 pints Beef Stock (see page 148)
1kg/2lb new potatoes, cubed
Salt and freshly ground black pepper
Sour cream, to garnish

• Melt half the butter or lard in a large, heavy-bottomed pan. Add the meat and stir over high heat until uniformly browned, then remove. Pour the excess juices and fat from the meat back into the pan, add the remaining butter, then fry the onions over medium heat with the garlic, caraway, chillies and paprika.
• When the onions have softened, stir in the flour until well incorporated – this will soak up the excess fat – then the peppers and tomatoes and fry for a few more minutes. Meanwhile, heat up the stock in a separate pan and add it to the vegetables, then the beef, and finally the potatoes.
• Cover and simmer over low heat for 1½–2 hours, until the meat is tender. Add a little water if sticking. Season to taste and serve with sour cream on the side.
SERVES 6-8

POLISH BLUEBERRY WITH APRICOT COMPOTE

THE SOUP
750g/1½lb fresh
    blueberries
600ml/1 pint water
150g/5oz soft brown sugar
3 tbs plain flour
300ml/½ pint sour cream
½ tsp salt

THE COMPOTE
750g/1½lb stoned apricots
150g/5oz soft brown sugar

This heavenly fruit soup was created by Nick in a moment of divine inspiration. Having drawn a blank in his search for the sour cherries he required to make a classic Hungarian sour cherry soup, he decided to improvise. Then it turned out the Poles had secretly had the sense to make blueberry soup all along. Great minds think alike…

Central Europeans are great forest foragers, and the Poles love their blueberries. Whether or not they like apricots is a matter for conjecture, but we've decided to put them in anyway. They taste nice and sharp against the smooth, creamy blueberries, and also provide an interesting colour contrast to the almost luminous lilac background. This is real stick-your-face-in-the-bowl stuff, and very rich, so you don't need much.

• Place the blueberries, water and sugar in a pan over medium heat and simmer for 10 minutes, stirring occasionally. Mix the flour, sour cream and salt in a bowl and whisk until smooth. Pour in one cup of the hot blueberry mix and whisk vigorously.
• Now add the mixture to the simmering blueberries, stir well and continue to simmer for 10 minutes until the soup thickens. Blend in a food processor, reserving a few blueberries for garnish. Transfer to a bowl and leave to cool with clingfilm resting on the surface to prevent a skin forming.
• To make the compôte, place the apricots and sugar in a pan over a low heat for about 45 minutes, or until the apricots are cooked through. Stir very gently, so that the apricots remain relatively whole. Transfer to a bowl and leave to cool in the fridge. The recipe makes far more than you need, but the compôte keeps well and, if you try some with yoghurt, you'll be glad you made the extra.
• Serve this velvety soup chilled, garnished with whole blueberries and a blob of compôte in the middle of each bowl. It works equally well as an unusual summer starter or as a dessert.
SERVES 4-6 (SMALL PORTIONS) [v]

The
Islamic
World

THE KORAN may impose various dietary restrictions on the faithful (notably the prohibition of pork and alcohol), but these if anything only serve to enhance the luxuriant sensual pleasure which typifies North African and Middle Eastern cooking. One whiff of a souk or bazaar is enough to convince on this point, and to confirm the vital role that the region historically played in the great spice trail. In combination with the cultural premium placed on hospitality throughout the Islamic world (which makes a great deal of sense in the middle of a desert), this results in some mighty fine soups and stews.

The tradition of keeping women in the home may be on the wane in some parts of the region, but it has certainly had an important effect on the character of Islamic soups. Slow cooking is the norm, with little place for underdone vegetables or red meat, and soups are often cooked for so long that it is impossible to distinguish the constituent ingredients. Soup-making is a communal activity, as is its consumption. Whole-meal soups dominate, and many play an important role in religious festivals, such as weddings (there are many specifically designated 'wedding soups') and Ramadan (see recipe for Moroccan Lamb Stew with Harissa on page 50).

As might be expected in one of the hottest sections of the globe, chilled soups have a very important role in the Islamic world. Cooling yoghurt is particularly prominent, and liquid food has an irresistible logic when the mercury threatens to boil. But it can get decidedly chilly in arid areas at high altitudes and in winter, and early morning street vendors selling steaming breakfast soups with Arab or pitta bread are a common sight in the towns of North Africa and the Middle East.

The difficulty of storing fresh meat in a hot climate has played its part in making the area a paradise for vegetarians. Even the humble parsley is elevated to the status of a vegetable. Particularly important are vegetables amenable to being kept in dried form, such as lentils (which have more protein per gram than sirloin steak) and pulses. The local love of pulses has produced an entire category of beautiful creamy soups, voluptuously enhanced with rich and delicate spices, lemon, garlic and fresh herbs.

Tradition is a powerful force in the Islamic world. The recipes for many of the most popular soups remain essentially unchanged from those prescribed in mediaeval texts, although *samna* (clarified butter) and olive oil have largely superceded the melted tail of the fat-tailed sheep as the basic starting points for soups and stews.

One Middle Eastern cookery writer summed up the prevailing attitude to soup in the region when he said, with reference to the great Persian poet Omar Khayyam: 'Let Omar sing of wine and bread. Myself, I prefer soup instead'. We hope the following recipes will make you see where he was coming from.

ISLAMIC FISH AND CHICKPEA STEW

300g/11oz dried chickpeas

1.5 litres/2²/3 pints Chicken
   Stock (see page 147)

4 red peppers

6 medium tomatoes

75ml/3fl oz olive oil

125g/4oz leeks, chopped

125g/4oz celery, chopped

150g/5oz onion, chopped

½ tsp cumin

4 cloves garlic, chopped

2 medium red chillies,
   chopped and de-seeded

Pinch of cinnamon

Salt and freshly ground
   black pepper to season

4 sea bass fillets, descaled

½ tsp paprika

1 bunch mint, chopped

1 bunch basil, chopped

1 bunch flat leaf parsley,
   chopped

Juice of 1 lemon

Nutty chickpeas and copious quantities of fresh herbs are responsible for the Islamic qualities of this dish, rather than the fish themselves, which can be any religion you like. We have chosen to use sea bass, but fresh sardines would make an excellent substitute.

• Soak the chickpeas overnight, then drain off the water and simmer them in the chicken stock for up to 3 hours, until quite soft.
• Roast the peppers and tomatoes in a hot oven (230°C/450°F/gas 8) for about half an hour, peel and de-seed the peppers and reserve both.
• Fry the leek, celery, onion, cumin, garlic and chillies in the olive oil until soft. Drain the stock from the chickpeas and pour it over the vegetables with the cinnamon, adding the roasted peppers and tomatoes. Blend this mixture together with about twenty per cent of the chickpeas. Return to a slow simmer, adding the remaining, intact chickpeas.
• Coat the sea bass fillets with the paprika, salt and black pepper, and score them slightly on the skin side. This will prevent them curling as you fry them for 2 minutes on each side over moderate heat in a non-stick pan. While you are doing this, add the chopped herbs to the stew – doing this at the last minute ensures maximum flavour.
• Serve with a fish fillet atop each portion of the soup, and sprinkle with the lemon juice.
SERVES 4 WITH SOME TO SPARE [G][L][D]

SQUASH WITH MINT PUREE

This simple and delicious soup can be served either hot or cold, and is made what it is by a tangy mint purée. Other things being equal, we prefer to use courgettes rather than marrows as they are less watery and have a more concentrated flavour.

THE SOUP
800g/1³/₄lb marrow or
   courgette
salt and black pepper
25ml/1fl oz olive oil
150g/5oz onion, sliced
125g/4oz celery, sliced
800ml/1¹/₂ pints
   Vegetable stock (see
   page 147)

THE PUREE
75ml/3fl oz olive oil
125g/4oz fresh mint,
   stalks discarded
juice of 1 lemon
1 tsp caraway seed
2 red chillies,
   deseeded
3 cloves of garlic
150ml/5fl oz plain
   yoghurt to garnish

- Drizzle the marrow or courgettes with olive oil, season them and bake in an oven pre-heated to 220°C/425°F/gas 7 for 30 minutes.
- Sweat the onion and celery in 25ml/1fl oz olive oil, then add the vegetable stock and the roasted marrow/courgettes. Simmer for a couple of minutes, season to taste, then blend.
- Blend all the ingredients for the mint purée, and garnish each portion of soup with a blob of this and a dollop of yoghurt.

SERVES 4-6 [V][L][G]

MOROCCAN LAMB WITH HARISSA AND GREEN LENTILS

Harissa is a paste heavily laden with red chillies, garlic and olive oil, which Moroccans love to add to their food. It is often squeezed from a tube, though that would not be our way.

This stew is a particular favourite during Ramadan. As the sun goes down, its fragrant, spiced aroma draws people into the souks in eager anticipation of breaking their fast.

THE HARISSA
2 tbs cumin seeds
2 red chillies
50g/2oz flat-leaf
   parsley
50g/2oz mint
50g/2oz basil
6 cloves garlic
5 tbs olive oil
¹/₂ tsp salt
¹/₂ tsp black pepper
5 tbs freshly squeezed
   lemon juice

THE STEW
3 red peppers
50ml/2fl oz olive oil
375g/12oz lamb, diced
250g/8oz onions,
   chopped
125g/4oz celery, chopped
1.5 litres/2¹/₂ pints
   Lamb Stock (see
   page 149)
300ml/¹/₂ pint passata
250g/8oz green lentils
Salt and freshly ground
   black pepper

TO GARNISH
Chopped mint
Chopped parsley
1 tbs lemon juice

- Preheat the oven to 220°C/425°F/gas 7. Roast the peppers (see page 156), skin, core, de-seed, cut into slices and reserve.
- Toast the cumin seeds for a few minutes in the hot oven, then blend all the ingredients for the harissa in a food processor until completely puréed. This takes a few minutes.
- Heat the olive oil in a large pan, add the lamb and stir continuously until lightly browned. Add the onion and celery and continue to fry on moderate heat for 5 minutes. Meanwhile, heat up the stock in a separate pan. Add the harissa to the lamb and continue to cook for a few minutes, then pour in the passata, hot stock and lentils. Season with salt and pepper. Cook slowly for 1¹/₂ hours, stirring occasionally. Add water if it becomes too thick. The oil that collects on the surface can be skimmed off if desired, but this would raise eyebrows in Marrakesh.
- Before serving, sprinkle with chopped mint, parsley and lemon juice. Arab or pitta bread are the ideal accompaniments.

SERVES 4-6 [D][G]

COLD YOGHURT
WITH BAKED COURGETTES

THE SOUP

300ml/½ pint Greek yoghurt

25ml/1fl oz olive oil

25g/1oz wholegrain
mustard

3 cloves garlic

125ml/4fl oz double cream

½ tsp caraway seeds

800ml/1⅓ pints Vegetable
or Chicken Stock (see
page 147)

1–2 small red chillies,
deseeded

THE GARNISH

1 large aubergine

750g/1½lb courgettes

Olive oil

Salt and freshly ground
black pepper

1 bunch chives, chopped

1 tsp paprika

Zest of 1 lemon

Yoghurt only began to play a significant role in the eating habits of the West during this century, when a biologist from the Pasteur Institute in Paris identified it as a major factor in the startling longevity of groups he studied in the Balkans and Caucasian Mountains. This would have come as no surprise to inhabitants of the Muslim world, who have been thriving on the stuff for millennia.

- Blend all the ingredients for the soup in a food processor and refrigerate.
- Preheat the oven to 230°C/450°F/gas 8. Place the aubergine and courgettes in a roasting tin and sprinkle with a little olive oil, salt and pepper. Bake for 20 minutes at the most – this should brown them on the outside and seal in the juices. Alternatively, char-grill them for a few minutes. Allow to cool before serving.
- Just before serving, cut the aubergine into chunks, slice the courgettes and stir into the soup. Sprinkle with the chives, paprika and lemon zest.

SERVES 4-6 [G][OPTIONALLY V]

NORTH AFRICAN SPINACH SOUP

This was a pretty popular soup at our cafés. The key is to make it as fresh as possible, in order to preserve the taste of the herbs and prevent it fading from green to a less appetising brownish colour. Although thoroughly righteous (no meat, dairy products or gluten) it is wholesome and aromatic.

- Heat the olive oil in a large pan. Add the onions with the garlic, paprika, chilli, caraway seed and a little of the mint and parsley, and fry until softened. Meanwhile, heat up the vegetable stock in a separate pan. Add the vegetable stock and simmer for 10 minutes.
- Add the spinach, the remaining herbs, and the lemon juice and zest, and purée the soup briefly in a food processor, leaving it quite textured. Serve immediately, garnished with a little Greek yoghurt if it takes your fancy.

SERVES 4-6 [D][G][L][V]

2 tbs olive oil

250g/8oz red onions, sliced

2 cloves garlic, chopped

1 tsp paprika

½ tsp chopped red chilli

1½ tsp caraway seed

1 bunch (about 50g/2oz) mint, chopped

1 bunch (about 50g/2oz) flat-leaf parsley, chopped

1 litre/1¾ pints Vegetable Stock (see page 147)

500g/1lb fresh spinach, finely chopped

Juice of 2 lemons

Zest of 1 lemon

Greek yoghurt, to garnish, (optional)

VEGETABLE HARIRA WITH COUSCOUS

THE COUSCOUS

250g/8oz couscous

1 tbs olive oil

Vegetable Stock (see
   page 147) to soak
   the couscous

2 tbs lemon juice

Salt and freshly
   ground black pepper

THE HARIRA

1 head of garlic

Salt and freshly
   ground black pepper

3–4 tbs olive oil

5 medium tomatoes

25g/1oz basil

25g/1oz mint

25g/1oz flat-leaf
   parsley

2 red chillies, chopped
   and deseeded

Juice of 1 lemon

1 tsp cumin seed

175g/6oz carrots,
   chopped

125g/4oz leeks, chopped

125g/4oz celery,
   chopped

250g/8oz shallots,
   chopped

1.25 litres/2 pints
   Vegetable Stock (see
   page 147)

2 red peppers, roasted,
   skinned, cored, de-
   seeded and chopped

250g/8oz French beans,
   sliced

250g/8oz frozen petit
   pois

mint leaves, to garnish

This Moroccan vegetable stew is great. We'll say no more –
just try it.

• Coat the couscous with the olive oil, and soak it in boiling, seasoned
vegetable stock with the lemon juice, following the instructions on the
packet. Preheat the oven to 200°C/400°F/gas 6.
• Cut the top off the head of garlic, season with salt and pepper and
drizzle with olive oil. Wrap the garlic in foil and place in a roasting
tin. Place the tomatoes in the tin and drizzle with olive oil. Roast the
garlic and tomatoes in the oven for 20 minutes (see page 156).
• Squeeze the garlic purée out of its skin. Blend in a food processor
with the roasted tomatoes, the basil, mint, parsley, chillies, cumin seed
and 1 tablespoon of olive oil. Put the mixture aside.
• Heat the remaining olive oil in a large, heavy pan. Add the carrots,
leeks, celery and shallots and fry gently until softened. Meanwhile,
heat up the stock in a separate pan. Add the stock to the fried
vegetables and bring to the boil. Add the peppers, beans and peas and
simmer for 5 minutes. Now stir in the puréed herbs and lemon juice
and simmer for 2–3 minutes. An aromatic oily film will rise to the
surface, which is good and to be expected. Serve the soup with a pile
of couscous in the middle of each bowl.
SERVES 6 [v][d][g][l]

FRUITY CHICKEN

This mellow, slow-cooked soup features apricots and a host of typically Islamic ingredients. It is particularly good served with plain couscous.

1 small bunch mint, roughly chopped
1 small bunch flat-leaf parsley, roughly chopped
1 small bunch basil, roughly chopped
1 small bunch coriander, roughly chopped
Juice of 2 lemons
4 cloves garlic
1 tsp ground cumin
1 tbs medium, deseeded and chopped red chillies
1 tsp paprika
1 tsp turmeric
1/2 tsp ground cinnamon
125ml/4fl oz olive oil
425g/14oz chicken fillets, skinned and sliced
200g/7oz onion, sliced
150g/4oz celery
6 tomatoes, peeled, deseeded and chopped
50g/2oz plain flour
1.5 litres/2 1/2 pints Chicken Stock (see page 147)
200g/7oz dried apricots
1 x 400g/14oz tin of chickpeas, drained
Salt and freshly ground black pepper

• Purée the mint, parsley, basil and coriander in a food processor with the lemon juice, garlic, cumin, chillies, paprika, turmeric and cinnamon and 50ml/2fl oz of the olive oil. Pour into a shallow dish, add the chicken and turn to coat. Leave to marinate for 1–2 hours.
• Remove the chicken from the marinade, shaking off any excess, and reserve the marinade. Heat 25ml/1fl oz of the olive oil in a large pan and add the chicken. Fry on all sides over a medium heat until evenly browned, then remove and reserve.
• Add the remaining olive oil to the pan and fry the onion and celery over a medium heat. Add the tomatoes and the reserved marinade and cook for 5 minutes, stirring frequently. Stir in the flour until thoroughly incorporated, then add the stock, apricots, chicken and chickpeas and simmer for 30 minutes.
• Season to taste and serve with plain couscous.
SERVES 6 [D]

COLD SPICY TOMATO WITH MINT, PARSLEY AND BASIL

This extremely healthy soup is essentially a liquid salad, given a zesty kick with the lemon juice and skin and the chillies. The tomatoes are the only cooked item, slow baked with olive oil, brown sugar and balsamic vinegar to give a sweet intensity to the finished soup. Cherry tomatoes are not cheap, but they give the best results, and don't be shy with the herbs.

800g/1lb 10oz cherry tomatoes
2 tsp brown sugar
125ml/4fl oz balsamic vinegar
125ml/4fl oz olive oil
800ml/1 1/3 pints Chicken or Vegetable Stock (see page 147)
3 slices stale bread, roughly chopped
1/2 cucumber, roughly chopped
1 bunch basil
1 bunch flat-leaf parsley
1 bunch mint
Juice and zest of 1 lemon
3 red chillies, chopped and deseeded
3 cloves garlic, chopped
1 tsp paprika
Salt and freshly ground black pepper

• Preheat the oven to 150°C/300°F/gas 2. Place the tomatoes in a roasting tin and sprinkle with the brown sugar, balsamic vinegar and olive oil. Bake for 1 1/2–2 hours.
• Add the tomatoes to the remaining ingredients and blend, either with a hand blender in a large bowl or in batches in a food processor, until thick and emulsified. Chill in the fridge for a couple of hours before serving.
• Serve with ciabatta bread and a mozzarella side salad.
SERVES 4-6 [L][D][OPTIONALLY V]

India

ALTHOUGH the characteristic spices and flavours of India make for some excellent soups, the truth is that the Indians are not, on the whole, a great nation of soup eaters. There are, however, some glorious exceptions to the general rule. Perhaps the best known is mulligatawny, British in concept but thoroughly Indian in execution, which the Anglo-Indian community has been joyfully wolfing down for the last 300 years.

The fact that genuine Indian soups are relatively thin on the ground need not provide an insuperable barrier to the creative soup lover. In the first place, what soups there are tend to be absolute gems, such as rasam, an exquisite tamarind-flavoured lentil broth from the South. Secondly, following the lead provided by mulligatawny, it is possible to come up with many highly successful 'translations' of the essence of Indian cuisine into the realm of soup. Chicken tikka, for example, is probably the most popular dish in the UK bar none, and it only takes a little imagination to transform the basic recipe into a terrific soup.

Indian cooking is more diverse than Western curry houses would suggest. In a country with an area similar to that of Western Europe and some two and a half times as many people, it could scarcely be any other way. Geographical, climatic, ethnic and religious variations all feed directly through into the kinds of food eaten and the way they are prepared. Nevertheless, one philosophy underpins the eating habits of at least the eighty per cent of the population that adheres to Hinduism. This is the Ayurvedic philosophy (the word roughly translates as 'knowledge of life span'), an ancient body of wisdom concerned with health, both physical and spiritual, the meaning of life and the way to enlightenment.

According to the Ayurveda, the health of the body depends on the balance of the three vital life forces or 'humours' it is believed to contain. This balance is directly influenced by the six basic tastes – sweet, sour, salty, pungent, bitter and astringent – each of which has a specific therapeutic action. A lack of any of these in the diet will aggravate the relevant humour. The consequence of this belief is that Ayurveda-influenced Indian meals tend to be rich and complex affairs, with care taken to ensure that all the fundamental tastes are represented. Food is further classified as *Satvic* (pure, simple and spiritual), *Rajasic* (worldly and spicy) or *Tamsic* (oily and lugubrious), as are the people who eat it.

The soups that follow are not guaranteed to catapult you to enlightenment, but they do embody some of the subtlety and concern for health which the Indians have been honing for millennia, as well as some of the spiciness. With India set to overtake China as the world's most populous nation at some point in the twenty-first century, it is high time this ancient knowledge was applied to soup.

CHICKEN TIKKA SOUP

THE MARINADE

125ml/4fl oz plain yoghurt

2 tsp chopped root ginger

2 tsp chopped garlic

1 tsp chopped red chilli

1 tsp paprika

1 tsp turmeric

1/2 tsp white pepper

1/2 tsp ground cumin

1/2 tsp ground cardamom

1/2 tsp salt

1/4 tsp ground mace

1/4 tsp ground nutmeg

THE SOUP

600g/1¼ lb chicken fillets,
  cut into big chunks

50g/2oz butter or ghee

200g/7oz onions, chopped

1 tsp chopped red chilli

1 tsp chopped root ginger

1 tsp chopped garlic

1 tbs garam masala

1 litre/1¾ pints Chicken
  Stock (see page 147)

50g/2oz plain flour

200g/7oz cooked green lentils

125ml/4fl oz plain yoghurt,
  plus extra for drizzling

150ml/5fl oz double cream

1 small bunch coriander,
  chopped, a few leave
  reserved for garnish

Salt

Chicken Tikka is so popular in the UK that it has become one of the best-selling sandwich fillings in the country, something they certainly never envisaged in the Punjab. They probably didn't expect it to be turned into a soup either, but then they were reckoning without us.

• Blend all the ingredients for the marinade in a food processor. Spread it all over the chicken, rubbing it in thoroughly. Leave to marinate for 3 hours.
• Remove the chicken from the marinade and char-grill or barbecue for about 5–10 minutes on each side, until cooked through. Reserve the excess marinade for the soup.
• Melt the butter in a large pan, add the onions, chilli, ginger, garlic and garam masala, cover and sweat for 5 minutes. Meanwhile, heat up the stock in a separate pan. Add the excess marinade to the vegetables, stir in the flour and cook for 2–3 minutes. Add the chicken stock and the lentils, bring to the boil, simmer for a few minutes, then blend in a food processor.
• Return the soup to the pan and stir in the yoghurt, cream and most of the coriander. Season with salt to taste and serve, laying the chicken on top and sprinkling with coriander. Drizzle with a little extra yoghurt.
SERVES 4-6

RASAM

This warming South Indian soup is flavoured with lentil broth and tamarind pulp. Tamarind, which grows in the form of brown pods on a tree of the same name, has a distinctive sweet/sour taste and is much used as a souring agent. If you cannot get your hands on fresh pods, you can purchase the pulp in bottled form in Indian supermarkets.

500g/1lb ripe red tomatoes
200g/7oz onion, sliced
2 tsp cumin seeds
1 clove garlic, finely chopped
Salt and freshly ground black pepper
25ml/1fl oz olive or vegetable oil
200g/7oz yellow lentils
2 litres/3½ pints water
50g/2oz tamarind pulp
50g/2oz ghee (clarified butter) or butter
1 tsp deseeded and chopped red chillies
4 cloves
1 tsp chopped root ginger
2 tsp ground coriander
1 tsp turmeric
1 small bunch fresh coriander, chopped

- Preheat the oven to 200°C/400°F/gas 6. Place the tomatoes in a baking dish with the onion, cumin, garlic and a little salt and pepper and drizzle with the oil. Bake for 30 minutes, then blend (either in a food processor or with a stick blender) and reserve.
- Place the lentils with the water in a large pan and boil for 45 minutes, or until tender. Blend in a food processor, and leave to stand until the solid lentil pulp has sunk to the bottom. Ladle off the liquid broth from the top, to obtain at least 1 litre/1¾ pints, and keep the pulp for use in another dish.
- Pour 50ml/2fl oz boiling water over the tamarind pulp and mash it hard. Squeeze the juice through a sieve, discarding the matted pulp.
- Melt the ghee or butter in a large, heavy pan over a low heat and add the chillies, cloves, ginger, ground coriander and turmeric. Stir for 2–3 minutes, then add the tomato mix, lentil broth, tamarind juice, chopped coriander and seasoning to taste and heat gently until warmed though.
- Serve with plenty of basmati rice.

SERVES 6 [V][G]

MULLIGATAWNY

Mulligatawny gets its name from the Tamil for 'peppery water', a rather gloomy verdict on this excellent and extremely popular Anglo-Indian soup.

75g/3oz butter
250g/8oz onion, sliced
200g/7oz carrot, diced
2 cloves garlic, chopped
1 tsp ginger, chopped
4 cloves
4 cardamom seeds
1 tsp ground cumin
1 tsp ground coriander
1 tsp garam masala
1 tsp cayenne pepper
½ tsp ground white pepper
425g/14oz chicken fillets, skinned and cut into small chunks
125g/4oz finely ground almonds
1.25 litres/2 pints Chicken Stock (see page 147)
Salt, to taste
1 small bunch coriander, finely chopped
125ml/4fl oz Greek yoghurt
125ml/4fl oz double cream

- Melt the butter in a large, heavy pan over medium heat. Add the onion, carrot, garlic, ginger, cloves, cardamom, cumin, ground coriander, garam masala, cayenne and white pepper and fry for about 5 minutes, stirring constantly to make sure the spices don't stick to the pan.
- Add the chicken and stir-fry until it starts to brown. Add the ground almonds and the stock, cover and simmer for 40 minutes.
- Add salt to taste, stir in the yoghurt and cream, and simmer over low heat for 1 more minute to heat through. Garnish with coriander and serve with a large bowl of basmati rice.

SERVES 4-6 [G][N]

SPICY MANGO LASSI

Lassi is the original drinking yoghurt, and is consumed with relish all over India. The same could be said for mangoes, which come in hundreds of varieties on the sub-continent, graded according to sweetness, texture and perfume. They've been growing mangoes for 4000 years, and so have had plenty of time to work out what to do with them. Don't be scared by the chilli element in the recipe below – it works rather in the way pepper does with strawberries, or that dash of Tabasco in your Bloody Mary, enhancing rather than overwhelming the surrounding sweetness.

• Blend all the ingredients together in a food processor, chill and serve in tall glasses or soup bowls, garnished with the red chilli.

SERVES 4 [V][G]

2 large ripe mangoes, peeled and diced, plus extra for garnish
1 red chilli, deseeded and chopped, plus extra for garnish
450ml/3/4 pint plain or Greek yoghurt
1 tbs clear honey (adjust according to sweetness of mango)
1 tbs lime juice
300ml/1/2 pint semi-skimmed milk

HOT YOGHURT SOUP

This soup is healthy, hot and, well, yoghurty. It will probably make you live for a very long time.

• Melt the ghee or butter in a large, heavy pan over a medium heat. Add the onions, garlic, cumin, coriander, cinnamon, nutmeg, ginger, cloves, chillies and cardamom and fry for 5 minutes, stirring frequently. Add the lentils and stir thoroughly for 5 minutes. Meanwhile, heat up the stock in a separate pan.

• Pour in the hot stock, bring to the boil and simmer for 1 hour. Drop in the spinach, and simmer for 5 minutes.

• Mix the cream and Greek yoghurt together and stir into the soup. Heat gently for 1 minute and season to taste. Serve with plenty of naan bread and basmati rice.

SERVES 4-6 [V][G]

50g/2oz ghee (clarified butter) or butter
200g/7oz onion, chopped
3 cloves garlic, chopped
1 tsp cumin seed
1 tsp ground coriander
Pinch of ground cinnamon
Pinch of ground nutmeg
1 tsp chopped root ginger
1/2 tsp ground cloves
1 tsp deseeded and chopped red chillies
1/2 tsp ground cardamom
200g/7oz green lentils
1.25 litres/2 pints Vegetable Stock (see page 147)
500g/1lb spinach, finely chopped
125ml/4fl oz double cream
125ml/4fl oz Greek yoghurt
Salt and freshly ground black pepper

LAMB PASSANDA WITH SPINACH

This creamy, delicate, spicy stew is a wonderfully exotic thing to do with lamb. Ideally, you would serve it with naan bread and basmati rice.

1 tsp chopped and deseeded red chilli
1 tsp chopped garlic
1 tsp chopped root ginger
Juice of 1 lemon
125ml/4fl oz plain yoghurt
600g/1¼lb lamb leg fillet, cut into 2.5cm/1in chunks
50ml/2fl oz olive oil
200g/7oz onions, sliced
1 tsp toasted cumin seeds
6 cardamom seeds
6 cloves
1 tbs garam masala
50g/2oz ground almonds
50g/2oz powdered coconut reconstituted in 200ml/7fl oz Lamb Stock (see page 149) or 1 x 400g/14oz tin of coconut milk
800ml/1⅓ pints Lamb Stock (see p. 149)
Salt to taste
425g/14oz fresh spinach, chopped
1 small bunch coriander, chopped

• Mix half the chilli, garlic and ginger, all the lemon juice and all the yoghurt in a shallow dish. Add the lamb, turn to coat and leave to marinate for 1 hour.
• Heat the olive oil in a large pan. Remove the lamb (reserving the marinade) and fry over high heat in the oil until browned and sealed. Add the onion, cumin, cardamom, cloves, garam masala and the remaining chilli, ginger and garlic, and fry gently for about 10 minutes, stirring continuously to prevent it sticking.
• Now add the reserved yoghurt marinade and cook for 2–3 minutes more before stirring in the almonds, coconut milk, stock and a little salt. Bring to the boil, then reduce the heat, cover and simmer for 1 hour.
• Stir in the spinach and coriander, adjust the seaoning and simmer for 5 minutes before serving.
SERVES 4-6 [N][G]

DHAL WITH ROASTED TOMATOES

Dhal, the ubiquitous Indian lentil concoction, is here elevated into a soup. Green lentils have an earthy flavour and keep their shape better when cooked than their little red cousins. For maximum authenticity, this soup should be cooked in a battered and blackened saucepan over an open fire, but we'll understand if you'd rather use the stove.

75g/3oz butter
1 tsp garam masala
1 tsp turmeric
1 tsp cumin seed
1 tsp coriander seed
½ tsp ground nutmeg
1 tsp mustard seed
1 tsp deseeded chopped red chilli
1 tsp chopped root ginger
1 tsp chopped garlic
300g/10oz onions, sliced
375g/12oz green lentils
1.25 litres/2 pints Vegetable Stock (see page 147)
300ml/½ pint passata
Salt and freshly ground black pepper
300g/10oz cherry tomatoes
Dab of butter
250ml/8fl oz yoghurt, to garnish
2 tsp chopped coriander, to garnish

• Melt the butter in a large pan, add all the spices together with the chilli, ginger and garlic, and fry on low heat for a couple of minutes. Raise the heat to medium, add the onions, and stir continuously with a wooden spoon to prevent the spices from burning. When the onions start to soften, add the lentils and stir well to coat with the spices before adding the stock and the passata. Cover and cook slowly for 1–2 hours (the longer the tastier), adding water if the mixture threatens to dry out (which it might, lentils being exceedingly thirsty). You are aiming at a thickish, slushy texture. Add salt to taste.
• Preheat the oven to 150°C/ 300°F/gas 2. Place the cherry tomatoes in a roasting tin with salt and pepper and dot with the butter. Bake for 1 hour. They can either be mixed in with the cooked lentils or sat atop. Either way, garnish with a dab of yoghurt and a sprinkling of coriander before serving.
SERVES 4-6 [V][G]

Southeast Asia

IN RECENT YEARS, Thai food, with its aromatic blending of herbs, chilli, garlic and lemon flavours, has soared in popularity to the extent that it is now posing a real challenge to the traditional place of Chinese and Indian cooking in the affections of Western diners. Hot on its heels are the cuisines of Malaysia, Vietnam, Laos, Cambodia and Burma, many of which are only now coming to the world's attention. For the soup fan, this is all very good news.

The French have long preferred to describe this part of the world as Indo-China, and from both a geographical and a culinary perspective, this description has a great deal to be said for it. The influences of Indian and Chinese cooking may be somewhat unequal in different parts of the region (Burma, for example, being much more influenced by India and much less by China than Vietnam), but the cooking of Southeast Asia bears the unmistakable hallmarks of both. In this neck of the woods, you are liable to be served noodles with your curries and vice versa.

It would, however, be a gross injustice to imply that Southeast Asian cooking was just a fusion of elements borrowed from the big boys next door. Features particularly well developed in the region include the use of coconut milk as the basis for luxurious soups and sauces, and an unrivalled way with aromatic and pungent herbs and spices. The result is one of the most distinctive cuisines on earth.

The similar climates, over-lapping histories and common geography of the countries of Southeast Asia have naturally made for a fairly unified eating culture. There is probably more to be said for dividing the soups of the area according to whether they originate in the mountainous and forested interior areas or in the coastal plains than there is for doing so on the basis of nationality. Mountain soups often have something of the jungle about them, featuring exotic, flavour-packed leaves, roots and bark. Soups from the coastal zones tend to have a more cosmopolitan feel, reflecting their buzzing populations and historical trade links. They also make exquisite use of the abundant seafood of the Andaman and South China Seas. Either way, the soups of Southeast Asia represent a bonanza for anyone who likes their food liquid and eaten from a bowl. They are also particularly good in the summer, reflecting the fact that they were specifically evolved to fit hot, humid climates.

THAI RED SHELLFISH CURRY

Buy the freshest seafood you can lay your hands on – this is a special occasion soup.

RED CURRY PASTE
10 bird's eye chillies
1 tsp ground coriander
1 tsp ground cumin
½ tsp freshly ground
  black pepper
6 cloves garlic, chopped
2 tbs lemongrass,
  chopped
1 bunch coriander
1 tbs shrimp paste
25g/1oz galangal,
  peeled and chopped
1 tbs soy sauce
6 lime leaves, chopped
THE SOUP
2kg/4lb fresh mussels
1 tbs sesame oil
2 cloves garlic, chopped
1 tbs red curry paste
1 x 400ml/14fl oz tin
  of coconut milk
600ml/1 pint Fish
  Stock (see p. 149)
200g/7oz aubergines
200g/7oz clam meat
  (preferably fresh)
150g/5oz scallops
200g/7oz mangetout
1 small bunch Thai
  basil, chopped
2 stalks lemongrass,
  roughly chopped
2 tbs nam pla
2 tbs soy sauce
3 spring onions, chopped
3 lime leaves

• Blend all the curry paste ingredients to a smooth paste in a food processor.
• Scrub the mussels carefully, scraping off any barnacles. Then steep in a bucket of water with a little flour sprinkled in it for 2–3 hours to cleanse them of sand. Make sure the shells are tightly closed, otherwise discard them. Drain the mussels and place in a pan with a tight-fitting lid. Add a splash of water, cover and boil over a high heat for 5-8 minutes. Remove from the heat and discard any which haven't opened. Remove the mussels from the shells and reserve, with their juices.
• Heat the sesame oil in a large pan over moderate heat. Add the garlic and fry for a few minutes until it starts to brown, but don't let it burn. Add a heaped tablespoon of the red curry paste, stir it in, and fry for 2–3 minutes. Pour in the coconut milk and stock, add the aubergines, cover and simmer for 15 minutes.
• Stir in the mussels, clams and scallops, add the remaining ingredients and simmer for another 10 minutes before serving.
SERVES 4-6 [D][N][G][L]

LIME SOUP WITH CHILLI GINGER GARLIC PRAWNS

This soup is reliant on a good fish stock, perhaps made richer by simmering with the prawn heads and shells for 20 minutes. It is ideal for dinner parties, particularly if you barbecue the prawns to give it that delectable smoky flavour.

5 cloves garlic,
  chopped
3 red chillies,
  deseeded and
  chopped
2 tsp chopped root
  ginger
2-3 tbs soy sauce
Juice of 4 limes
1 tbs sesame oil
8 large raw prawns
1.25 litres/2 pints Fish
  Stock (see page
  149)
1 tbs chopped galangal
10 lime leaves
4 lemongrass stalks,
  cut into lengths
8 baby corns, cut
  diagonally
1 tbs shrimp paste
2 tbs nam pla or nuac
  mam (fish sauce)
Coriander leaves, to
  garnish

• Mix half the garlic, chilli, ginger and soy sauce in a shallow dish. Add a dash of the lime juice and all of the sesame oil, add the prawns, turn to coat and leave to marinate.
• Heat the fish stock in a large pan. Add the remaining garlic, chilli, ginger and soy sauce with the galangal, lime leaves, lemongrass, baby corn, shrimp paste and nam pla. Simmer for 10 minutes.
• Barbecue the prawns, or cook in a frying pan on high heat for a couple of minutes on either side until nicely browned. Add the remaining lime juice to the soup, and serve with the prawns on top, sprinkled with the coriander leaves.
SERVES 4 [D][G][L]

VIETNAMESE BEEF NOODLE SOUP

We didn't expect to sell a great deal of this at the restaurants, but the trick turned out to be just to get people to try it. This soup is a real winner, with rich beef stock soured by lime and deepened by star anise (which tastes of aniseed, appropriately enough) providing a tangy backdrop to wafer-thin slices of beef and pleasingly chewy noodles. It is also, once you've made the stock, a doddle.

1.25 litres/2 pints Beef Stock (see page 148)

4 star anise

2-3 bird's eye chillies, deseeded and chopped in two

25g/1oz piece root ginger, chopped into 4–5 pieces

4 cloves

4 cloves garlic

2 tbs nam pla or nuoc mam (fish sauce)

5 lime leaves

500g/1lb lean beef, such as top rump, sliced very thinly

Juice of 2 limes

Soy sauce to taste

375g/12 oz beansprouts

25g/1 oz coriander leaves, chopped

5 spring onions, chopped

500g/1lb fresh noodles

• Heat up the beef stock in a large pan, and add the star anise, chillies, ginger, cloves, garlic, fish sauce and lime leaves. Simmer for 20 minutes or so, then strain.

• Return the stock to the pan, put back on the heat and add the remaining ingredients except the noodles. Simmer for 4–5 minutes. Meanwhile, cook the noodles in a separate pan of simmering water for 3–4 minutes, then drain. Portion the noodles into bowls, pour the soup on top and serve.

SERVES 4-6 [D]

SEAFOOD LAKSA

This creamy speciality of the Malay/Singapore peninsula is often eaten by the local inhabitants as a mid-morning snack, but it more than suffices as a meal in itself. In its home territory, this soup would be served with flat rice laksa noodles, but as they are seldom available abroad, we've substituted egg noodles.

THE PASTE

50g/2oz ground almonds

3 cloves garlic

25g/1oz root ginger, peeled and roughly chopped

3 stalks lemongrass, trimmed

2 tbs small dried prawns

2 tbs nam pla or nuoc mam (fish sauce)

4 red chillies, deseeded and chopped

1 tsp turmeric

1 tsp ground cumin

50g/2oz shallots, chopped

1 small bunch coriander, with roots, washed thoroughly and roughly chopped

1 tbs sesame oil

[continues opposite]

THE LAKSA

800ml/1¹⁄₃ pints Fish Stock (see page 149)

400g/14oz raw prawns, peeled and de-veined, heads and shells reserved

1 x 400ml/14fl oz tin of coconut milk

250g/8oz baby squid, cleaned and chopped

200g/7oz sugar peas

2 tbs soy sauce

Juice of 2 limes

300g/10oz beansprouts

500g/1lb dried egg noodles, cooked according to instructions on the packet

4 spring onions, chopped, to garnish

Coriander leaves, to garnish

- Blend all the ingredients for the paste in a food processor until smooth, and reserve.
- Heat up the fish stock in a large pan. Add the prawn heads and shells and simmer for 20 minutes to enrich it, then strain and reserve.
- Fry the paste in a large heavy pan over a low heat for 5 minutes, stirring constantly to prevent it burning. Add the hot stock and the coconut milk and simmer for 5 minutes.
- Add the prawns, squid and sugar peas and simmer for a further 5 minutes,. Meanwhile, cook the egg noodles in a separate pan. Pour the soy sauce and lime juice into the soup at the last minute, and throw in the beansprouts.
- Serve on a bed of noodles, garnished with spring onions and coriander leaves.

SERVES 4-6 [D][N]

TOM YUM WITH BABY SQUID

THE PASTE

4 tbs vegetable oil

50g/2oz bird's eye chillies, deseeded and chopped

50g/2oz garlic, chopped

50g/2oz shallots, chopped

50g/2oz dried prawns, pounded in a pestle and mortar

Pinch of sugar

THE SOUP

1 litre/1¾ pints Fish or Chicken Stock (see page 149 and 147)

4 lime leaves

125g/4 oz oyster mushrooms, chopped

2 bird's eye chillies, deseeded and chopped

2 lemongrass stalks, sliced

4 tbs nam pla or nuoc mam (fish sauce)

10 baby corns

250g/8oz mangetout

4 tbs lime juice

500g/1lb baby squid, sliced or whole

2 spring onions, chopped

Coriander leaves, to garnish

If you look at satellite images of the Earth at night, the brightest blobs of light emanate from the oilfields of Siberia and, bizarrely, from the seas of Southeast Asia. The latter are caused by squid boats. Shine a bright light in the right tropical waters at night, and the squid will begin to congregate like moths.

The passion of the people of this region for squid borders on the obsessive. An excellent and abundant source of protein, in Thailand you can even buy them dried and sugared on a stick, like surreal Gary Larson ice-creams. The following classic recipe makes full use of the sweetest and most succulent baby squid, and one taste should make it obvious why we have chosen to transliterate the Thai name as 'Tom Yum' rather than the less evocative alternative 'Tom Yam'.

- To make the paste, heat the oil in a frying pan, add the chillies, garlic and shallots and fry until they start to brown. Add the prawns and sugar and fry gently for a little longer. This paste can be stored in the fridge for a few weeks.
- To make the soup, heat the stock and 2 tablespoons of the paste in a large pan. Add all the ingredients except the lime juice and squid and simmer, covered, for 20 minutes. Add the squid and lime juice and simmer for another 2 minutes. Serve garnished with the spring onions and coriander.

SERVES 4-6 [D][G][L]

LEMONGRASS AND GALANGAL WITH THAI BASIL PUREE

This verdant puréed soup celebrates the distinctive herbs which Thai cooking is all about. It is very nearly vegetarian, but not quite.

THE PUREE
1 bunch Thai basil
2 tbs sesame oil
1 tbs lemon juice

THE SOUP
2 tsp shrimp paste
2 tbs sesame oil
3 cloves garlic
2 hot red chillies, deseeded and chopped
1/2 tsp ground cumin
6 stalks lemongrass
1 tsp galangal

1/2 tsp ground coriander
125g/4oz shallots, finely chopped
900ml/1/2 pints Chicken Stock (see page 147)
1 x 400ml/14fl oz tin of coconut milk
2 tbs nam pla
1 tbs soy sauce
Juice of 1 lime
1 tbs cornflour
75ml/3fl oz cream

• Blend the ingredients for the purée in a food processor until smooth, then transfer to a bowl and chill. Blend the shrimp paste, half the sesame oil, garlic, chillies, cumin, lemongrass, galangal and coriander in a food processor until extremely smooth.

• Heat the remaining oil in a pan. Add the shallots, cover and sweat over low heat for 5 minutes. Stir in the paste from the food processor and simmer for 5 more minutes on a very low heat, stirring frequently.

• Add all but 50ml/2fl oz of the stock, the coconut milk, nam pla, soy sauce, and lime juice and simmer for a further 10 minutes. Whisk the cornflour into the remaining stock and pour this mixture into the soup, stirring continuously. Blend the soup again, then return to the pan over heat and simmer for 5 minutes, until the soup has thickened. Add the cream, bring to the boil briefly. Serve drizzled with the Thai basil purée.

SERVES 4 [N]

THAI GREEN CHICKEN CURRY WITH COCONUT

THE PASTE

2 stalks of lemongrass,
   trimmed and chopped

8 small green chillies,
   deseeded and chopped

4 shallots, chopped

25g/1oz root ginger, peeled

5 cloves garlic, chopped

1 small bunch coriander,
   roots included, cleaned

1 tsp ground cumin

1 tsp ground coriander

8 lime leaves, chopped

2 tsp shrimp paste

1 tbs nam pla or nuoc
   mam (fish sauce)

1/2 tsp ground star anise

THE CURRY

200g/7oz baby aubergines,
   quartered

2 tbs mixed vegetable and
   sesame oils

1 x 400ml/14fl oz tin of
   coconut milk

300g/10oz chicken breast,
   skinned and thinly sliced

2 tbs nam pla or nuoc
   mam (fish sauce)

2 tbs soy sauce

500ml/17fl oz Chicken
   Stock (see page 147)

6 lime leaves

2 stalks lemongrass,
   roughly chopped

1 small bunch Thai basil,
   chopped

Thai curries are a great deal more liquid and soupy than their Indian counterparts, and this one is no exception. There are various ready-made curry pastes on the market and in Thailand you can buy them fresh by weight, but you will feel much more accomplished if you make your own (and doubly so if you grind your own spices). There isn't much more to be said – this is justifiably one of the most popular dishes in the world. Shrimp paste is available in Oriental supermarkets.

• Blend all the ingredients for the paste in a food processor until smooth, then reserve. The end product may be rather too much for one curry, but it will keep in the fridge for up to two weeks; this recipe is equally good with beef or fish.
• Preheat the oven to 230°C/450°F/gas 8. Place the quartered baby aubergines in a roasting tin and drizzled with the oil. Roast for 10 minutes in the hot oven, then remove from the oven and reserve.
• Spoon 25g/1oz of curry paste into a large pan over a medium heat and stir-fry for 2–3 minutes, stirring frequently. Add the coconut milk and simmer for 5 minutes, still stirring.
• Add the chicken and the nam pla and soy sauce, and cook slowly for 5 minutes. Then add the stock, lime leaves, lemongrass and aubergine and simmer for 2–3 more minutes.
• Stir in the Thai basil and serve immediately.
SERVES 4 [D][G][N]

INDONESIAN CHICKEN

Indonesia is made up of 1,400 islands, home to an extraordinary range of tribes and ethnic sub-groups, and it takes over five hours to fly by jet from one end to the other. But the diversity you might expect to find has been systematically repressed by a ruthless regime intent on cultural assimilation and homogenization. Fortunately, some splendid soups remain, such as this Sumatran speciality.

1 tbs sesame oil

2 red chillies, deseeded and chopped

2 cloves garlic, chopped

4 spring onions, chopped

1 litre/1¾ pints Chicken Stock (see page 147)

1 x 400ml/14fl oz tin of coconut milk

6 water chestnuts, peeled and sliced

2 tbs soy sauce

425g/14oz chicken fillets, sliced

300g/10oz fresh egg noodles

200g/7oz beansprouts

150g/5oz spinach, thoroughly washed

1 small bunch coriander, leaves separated from stems and chopped

• Heat the sesame oil in a large pan. Add the chillies, garlic and spring onions and fry until they start to brown slightly. Pour in the stock and coconut milk, bring to the boil, then reduce to a simmer.
• Add the water chestnuts and simmer for another 10 minutes. Then add the soy sauce and the chicken and simmer for a further 5 minutes, stirring occasionally. Meanwhile, cook the egg noodles in boiling water for 3–4 minutes, refresh them in cold water, drain and divide between 4 bowls.
• Add the beansprouts and spinach to the soup, stir and serve immediately, poured over the noodles. Garnish with the chopped coriander.

SERVES 4 [D][N]

China

IN CHINA, soups are typically served at the end of a meal. Nothing could better illustrate the profound gulf between the world's most populous nation and the West than this one simple fact. But this is only the tip of the iceberg. Almost everything about Chinese soup is gloriously different, and that spells fun and adventure for the devotee of the ladle.

In the first place, the shape of the floating items in Chinese soups is given far greater importance than in the West. This is partly a consequence of the imperative, in the absence of knives and forks, to present all food in chopstick-friendly bite-sized portions. But it is also the result of a great respect for the forms of the natural world. The ideal of many Chinese soups is that of a clear, deep mountain pool containing many intriguing items of nature – there is something almost mystical about the Chinese attitudes to soups.

A second striking feature of Chinese soups is the sheer diversity of ingredients used. With twenty-two per cent of the world's population but only seven per cent of its cultivatable land, there has always been pressure to make use of everything edible. Hence the frequent presence of exotic materials such as wood fungus, lotus roots and sharks' fins, which no-one could call user-friendly. The ultimate example is bird's nest soup, made from nests constructed by a species of swift from its own saliva. The difficulty of harvesting these nests from sheer cliff faces and the exhaustive cleaning required have made this soup a seriously prestigious item.

Another distinctive characteristic of Chinese soups is rooted in Taoism, with its meticulous concern for the harmonisation of *yin* (female, cold, receptive) and *yang* (male, hot, dynamic) elements. Balance is everything. All food, but particularly soup, is viewed from a medicinal and holistic position. Particular soups may be prescribed for all kinds of ailments, with the aim always being to redress an imbalance between *yin* and *yang* within the sufferer, thereby strengthening the all important *qi* (vital energy).

Moreover, the Chinese possess an expertise with noodles and pasta to rival the Italians, and often apply this know-how to their soups. Then there is the question of stock. The most revered form is superior stock, deemed important and delicious enough to be served on its own, free of charge, in Beijing restaurants. We won't even go into the tortuous process of water changes and clarifications with dark, then white, chicken meat its production entails. The good news is that many superb Chinese soups can be made with the basic chicken, and duck and pork stocks featured in our Stocks chapter, perhaps enhanced with the judicious addition of dried shrimps or mushrooms.

TRADITIONAL PORK RIB (BAK KUT TEH)

This one is a bit of an adventure, particularly if you follow the Chinese habit of serving it for breakfast along with strong black tea, steamed rice and chopped red chillies and garlic to garnish. While the makers of cornflakes needn't shake in their boots just yet, you will find it works very well at other meals too.

The list of ingredients may seem a little scary, but half an hour in a Chinese supermarket should sort you out, particularly if you ask for help. *Bak kut teh* is traditionally simmered in a clay pot.

1kg/2lb pork ribs, chopped into 5cm/2in sections
2 litres/3¹/2 pints Duck and Pork or Chicken Stock (see pages 149 and 147)
2 whole star anise
1 cinnamon stick
6 cloves garlic
10g/¹/3oz tang sheng (a white sliced root)
10g/¹/3oz fibrous ginseng root
10g/¹/3oz dried red date
10g/¹/3oz medlar – a small dried red fruit
1 bag claypot bak kut teh herbs (like a Chinese bouquet garni)
soy sauce, to taste
chopped red chillies, to garnish
chopped garlic, to garnish

• Place the ribs and stock in a large, heavy pot and bring to the boil, then reduce to a simmer, skimming any scum from the surface.
• Add all the ingredients except the claypot bak kut teh herbs and soy sauce, and simmer for 2 hours.
• Strain the stock, and return the soup to the pan with the ribs. Add the bag of herbs and soy sauce to taste and simmer for another 30 minutes.
• Remove the bag of claypot bak kut teh herbs and serve with the chillies and garlic, steamed rice and strong black tea.
SERVES 4-6 [D][G]

RESTORATIVE CHICKEN BROTH WITH PAK CHOI

If (and we admit it's a big if) you have access to a Chinese supermarket and the patience to watch a stockpot boil for a good 6 hours, you are in for a treat with this one. The herbs in question are a traditional mix, like a medicinal Oriental bouquet garni, and can be bought in 125g/4oz packets at many Chinese food shops and herbalists. Just ask for 'chicken soup herbs'. Their names, for the record, are *dang shen*, *fu ling*, *shan yao*, *yu zhu*, *da zao*, *gou qi zi*, *huang qi* and the unforgettable *long yan rou*. Some are dried red berries, others dried roots, others frankly anyone's guess, but they all double in size when cooked and impart a slightly pungent, aromatic flavour.

In Chinese medicine, this soup is designed to reduce heat in the body and restore *yin yang* balance, making it, like so many chicken soups, an excellent antidote to colds and flu.

1 large boiling chicken
2 litres/3¹/2 pints water
125g/4oz Chinese 'chicken soup' herbs
2 x 2.5cm/1in pieces of root ginger
Soy sauce, to taste
500g/1lb pak choi
Snipped chives, to garnish

• Place the chicken in a large stockpot with the water, add the herbs and ginger, and simmer for 6 hours, skimming off all scum to keep the soup clear. Do not allow the soup to come to the boil.
• Strain the stock, reserving the chicken breast, and return to the pan. Cut the chicken breast into shreds and add to the stock. Bring the stock to a simmer, add soy sauce to taste and the pak choi and cook for a minute or so before serving. Sprinkle with a few snipped chives.
SERVES 6-8 [L][D][G]

BEEF AND GREEN PEA

1kg/2lb chuck steak

1.25 litres/2 pints Chicken
    Stock (see page 147)

1 cinnamon stick

3 red chillies

2 cloves garlic

3 star anise

25g/1oz dried citrus peel,
    soaked and chopped

500g/1lb frozen petit pois

5 spring onions,chopped

1 red chilli, deseeded and
    finely chopped

Soy sauce

This soup is extremely warming, satisfying and simple. A tough old cut of beef will produce the maximum flavour. The cooking is long and slow, and involves a lot of skimming to produce the desired clarity.

• Place the meat and stock in a large pan with the cinnamon, chillies, garlic, star anise and citrus peel. Simmer for 2–3 hours, skimming at regular intervals to prevent the soup becoming cloudy.

• Remove the soup from the heat and strain, reserving the meat. When the meat has cooled, cut it into thin slices, or for an even more authentic end product, tease it into shreds. Return the soup to the pan on the heat and add the beef, peas and spring onions and chilli, plus soy sauce to taste. Simmer for a few more minutes and the soup is ready to serve. This is delicious served with noodles.

SERVES 6 [D][G]

CHINESE BROTH

Have you heard of the cabbage soup diet? It is an excruciatingly boring yet effective way of losing weight. The recipe consists of mounds of sliced cabbage, boiled in water with a few other vegetables. You eat it day in day out, and it doesn't matter how much you put away for the soup has few calories and no fat.

There must be a tastier way to lose weight, we decided. Reasoning that chicken stock makes for infinitely better soup than water, we chose this as our starting point. It also happens to be fat free, keeps well in the fridge and can be whipped out to make a tasty soup in less than ten minutes. With fresh green vegetables like pac choi and choi sum, flavoured with chilli, ginger and garlic, a recipe similar to Chinese broth seemed to be recommending itself. If you've ever wondered why so many Chinese people are slim with clear complexions, it's because they live on stuff like this.

- Pour the stock into a pan. Add the chilli, ginger, garlic and lemongrass. Simmer for five minutes.
- Add the corn, carrots, chickens and greens. Simmer on for 5 more minutes. Season with the soy and fish sauces.
- Place the noodles in a bowl, pour the hot broth over them, and the soup is ready to serve.

SERVES 2 [L]

1 litre/1¾ pints rich Chicken Stock (see pages 147)
1 tsp chopped red chilli
1 tsp chopped ginger
200g/7oz dried rice noodles, cooked as per packet instructions, then refreshed in cold water
Soy sauce and fish sauce, to taste
1 stalk of fresh lemongrass
10 baby corn, sliced
1 carrot, roughly grated
10 stalks of kai lan (Chinese broccoli) or other greens that take your fancy)
2 sliced chicken breasts

PRAWN AND PORK WONTON

THE SOUP

1.25 litres/2 pints Duck and
  Pork or Chicken Stock
  (see pages 149 and 147)

1 tsp chopped root ginger

1 tsp chopped garlic

2 spring onions, chopped

Soy sauce, to taste

Coriander leaves, to garnish

THE WANTONS

300g/10oz minced pork

1 tbs soy sauce

2 spring onions, finely
  chopped

1 tsp sesame oil

1 egg white

Pinch of salt

1 packet wanton skins
  (about 35–50)

250g/8oz small, peeled, raw
  prawns (or cooked if
  unavailable)

This is extremely popular both in China and abroad, but often disappoints in Western restaurants, largely due to stingy stuffing of the wontons. No such problems with our version. Incidentally, wonton skins are a standard item in the fridges of Chinese supermarkets.

• Heat the stock in a large pan with the ginger and garlic and leave to simmer.
• Mix all the ingredients for the wontons in a bowl, except for the prawns. Place a teaspoon of the mixture on each wonton skin along with an individual prawn. Wet the edges with a little water, pull up the sides and pinch together, making a parcel resembling a minature old-fashioned purse with the strings drawn tight. Bring a large pan of water to the boil and simmer the wontons in it until they float to the surface, the sign that they are done. Remove with a slotted spoon and drain.
• Add the wontons to the simmering broth with the spring onions, and add soy sauce to taste. Simmer for a couple of minutes and serve garnished with coriander leaves.
SERVES 6 [D]

NOODLE SOUP WITH CHINESE GREENS

The Chinese have a way with greens which is reflected in the numerous varieties they use in their cooking – *gai lan*, Chinese broccoli, *choi sam* and Chinese flowering cabbage to name but a few. Pak choi is a particularly fine example, and is thankfully sneaking into Western supermarkets more and more. The other day Nick wandered down into London's Chinatown and came back with a kilo of pea shoots, as delicious as any green vegetable you might hope to encounter. Whatever you choose to use in this excellently simple soup (and it could perfectly well be spinach), leave it until the last minute to maximise colour, flavour and vitamin content. As far as the noodles go, fresh is best, as ever, but dried will do fine if you can't find any.

1.25 litres /2 pints Duck and Pork or Chicken Stock (see pages 149 and 147)	• Place the stock in a large pan with the ginger and garlic and simmer for half an hour. Add the soy sauce a little at a time, constantly tasting until the flavour reaches the desired richness.
1 tbs chopped root ginger	
4 cloves garlic, halved	• Cook the noodles by steeping them in simmering water for 3–4 minutes if fresh or follow the instructions on the packet if dried. Drain and portion them out into ceramic bowls.
2-3 tbs soy sauce, to taste	
300g/10oz Chinese egg noodles	
500g/1lb mixed fresh greens	• Simmer the greens in the broth for 2–3 minutes, pour on top of the noodles and serve. **SERVES 4-6** [D][L]

CRAB, BABY CORN AND BEAN CURD

This is in another league entirely from the crab and sweetcorn soup beloved of Chinese takeaways.

1.25 litres/2 pints Chicken Stock (see page 147)	• Heat up the stock with the corn in a large pan. Add the ginger and garlic, and simmer for 10 minutes. Now add the sherry, sugar and cornflour, bring briefly to the boil, then reduce to a simmer.
300g/10oz baby corn	
1 tbs chopped root ginger	
2 cloves garlic, chopped	
1 tbs sherry	
1 tsp sugar	
2 tsp cornflour mixed with the same amount of water	• Whisk the egg with the sesame oil. Add the crab meat and bean curd to the broth, then slowly pour in the egg and sesame oil mix, stirring constantly, ensuring the broth is at a bare simmer. Remove from the heat, add the spring onion and a little soy sauce to taste, and serve. **SERVES 4-6** [D][L]
1 egg white	
1 tsp sesame oil	
250g/8oz white crab meat, preferably fresh	
300g/10oz bean curd, cut into small cubes	
2 spring onions, chopped	
Soy sauce, to taste	

Japan

THE JAPANESE life expectancy is among the longest in the world. This has a lot to do with a diet strikingly low in saturated fats, dairy products and red meat. But they also drink a lot of soup, which is where we come in.

Made up of mountainous islands and home to over 125 million people, Japan provides very limited scope for agriculture. What little space there is tends to be given over to paddy fields to fuel the national obsession with rice. The lack of available pasture is largely responsible for the fact that meat has only really entered the Japanese diet in the last 100 years. Cattle, for example, are usually forced to spend their entire lives in sheds. This needn't be as gloomy as it sounds: the legendary cows of Kobe (providers of the world's most expensive beef) are fed on beer and given a daily massage, the idea being to create a luxurious marbling by ensuring that fat is evenly distributed through their muscle.

The geographical restraints have had two major effects. The first has been to direct Japanese attention to the sea, with a resulting profusion of seafood in the markets that beggars belief. Delicious and mineral rich edible seaweeds are harvested on a grand scale. They are also cultivated, which leads on nicely to the second consequence of the geography: resourcefulness. The Japanese are masters at using ingredients that the rest of the world steadfastly ignores – burdock root is a prime example – and transforming them into exquisite foodstuffs. The distinctive character of Japanese food is enhanced by the fact that the country virtually cut itself off from the rest of the world from the mid-seventeenth to the mid-nineteenth centuries.

When it comes to soup, there are two main categories. Clear soups are served at the beginning of a meal, and traditionally contain three solid ingredients – the main event or 'host' (often chicken or seafood), a complementary 'guest' (perhaps slices of mushroom), and a final touch to add piquancy and colour, such as seeds, or shards of fragrant edible leaf. The aesthetics of the results are comparable to those of flower arranging. Thick soups, on the other hand, are typically dished up towards the end of a meal, and are more often than not based on miso (fermented soya, rice or barley). Either way, soups are served in beautiful, laquered wooden bowls with lids.

Almost all Japanese soups are based on *dashi*, a stock with a delicious smell of the sea, made from dried flakes of the bonito fish and kombu seaweed (kelp). Recipes for the two most important versions appear in the Stocks chapter (see pages 146-151), but most Japanese housewives use instant *dashi*, which is widely available in Oriental supermarkets in the West. For those of you without access to such stores, perfectly good if slightly less authentic versions of the recipes that follow can be made with light chicken or vegetable stocks.

CLEAR SOUP WITH SCALLOPS

This light, refreshing soup with its succulent, barely cooked scallops epitomises the delicacy and simplicity which Japanese clear soups are all about.

2 tbs ginger juice (see below)

1 litre/1¾ pints Light Dashi (see page 150)

Pinch of salt

2 tbs tamari (light soy sauce)

2 tbs mirin

125g/4oz shiitake mushrooms, thinly sliced

4 large scallops

• To make the ginger juice, either freeze and then grate a large knob of ginger or chop and blend in a food processor. Either way, squeeze the resulting pulp through a fine sieve, catching the juice underneath.

• Place the dashi in a pan with the salt, tamari, mirin and ginger juice and simmer over moderate heat for 2–3 minutes. Stir the shiitake into the soup and cook for 5 minutes. Just before serving, slice the scallops thinly and add them to the soup, cooking for a matter of seconds before serving.

SERVES 4 [L][D][G]

CLEAR SOUP WITH SHIITAKE AND TOFU

The Japanese cultivate shiitake mushrooms via a highly complicated process that involves sewing the microscopic mycelium (roots) deep inside logs of freshly cut oak. The logs are then left in the forest, where they will produce a crop of mushrooms every spring and autumn for up to five years, until they rot completely. The fresh tofu in this recipe will soak up the flavour of the broth and provides a lovely, silky texture.

1.25 litres/2 pints Light Dashi (see page 150)

2 tbs soy sauce

6 spring onions, chopped

2 tbs mirin

2 tbs finely chopped root ginger

200g/7oz shiitake mushrooms, extremely thinly sliced

300g/10oz tofu, cut into small cubes

• Heat up all the ingredients in a large pan, apart from the tofu, and simmer for 5 minutes.

• Add the tofu, simmer for another 2–3 minutes, and serve.

SERVES 4 [L][D][G]

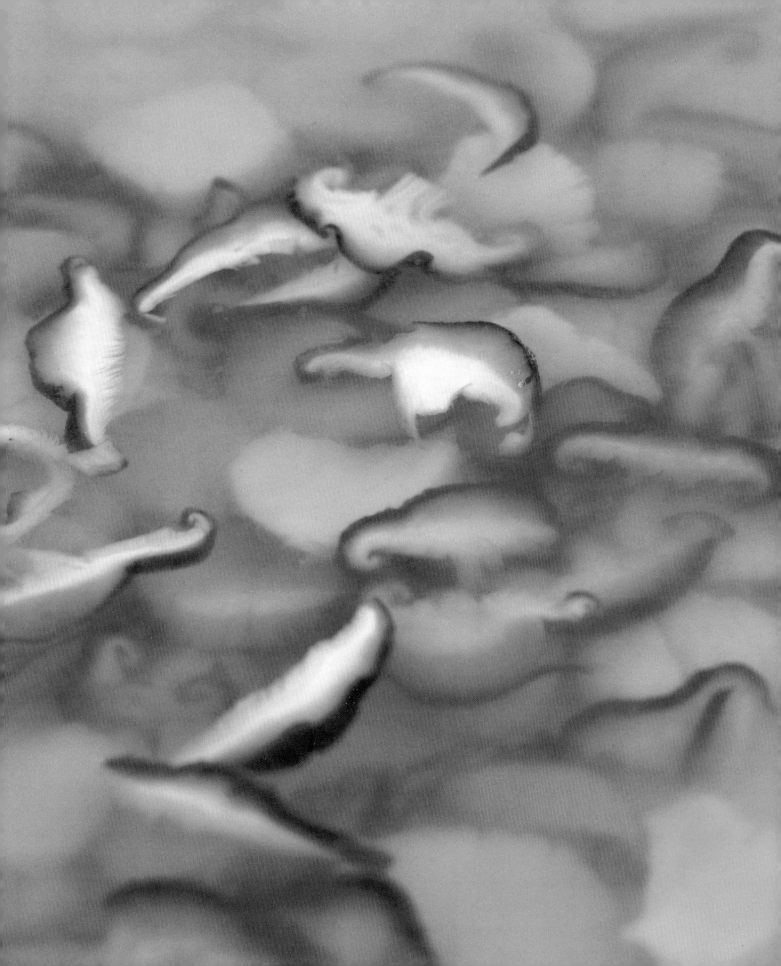

NOODLE SOUP WITH MACKEREL AND SPINACH

Simplicity is a feature of much of the best Japanese cooking. In this example, the soy sauce and the sharp taste of the ginger and spring onions cut through the oiliness of the mackerel to delicious effect.

250g/8oz fresh noodles
1 litre/1¾ pints light
    Dashi (see page 150)
5cm/2in piece root
    ginger, peeled and
    sliced lengthwise
250g/8oz young leaf
    spinach
4 mackerel fillets, cut
    into pieces and
    grilled
2 tbs soy sauce
1 spring onion,
    cut into shreds and
    soaked in cold water
    to make curls

• Cook the noodles in boiling water for 3–4 minutes, drain and set aside.
• Put the dashi in a pan, add the ginger and simmer for 5 minutes. Add the spinach and simmer for a few minutes until it has wilted. Mix in the soy sauce. Spoon the spinach and dashi mixture into bowls, add the noodles, and place the grilled mackerel on top, skin-side up. Garnish with the drained spring onion curls and serve.

SERVES 4 [D][L]

MISO SOUP WITH DAIKON, PORK AND SOBA NOODLES

This is robust Japanese country fare, and with pleasing symmetry, the recipe was taught to Nick by a robust Japanese country chef. Daikon is a kind of giant white radish, while mirin is a sweet cooking sake. If you can't get hold of the genuine articles, you can use mooli (a Pakistani variety of giant radish) or a handful of regular red radishes to replace the daikon, and cooking sherry to replace the mirin. Similarly, you can experiment with alternative noodles if you can't find any soba. Burdock roots may prove more troublesome: your options are to find a Japanese supermarket, do a bit of al fresco foraging (they grow wild in the UK) or do without them altogether.

200g/7oz dried soba
    noodles
1.25 litres/2 pints
    Heavy Dashi (see
    page 150)
1 small daikon, cut
    into very small strips
125g/4oz carrot, cut
    into very thin strips
2 burdock roots, cut
    into very thin strips
250g/8oz belly pork,
    very thinly sliced
125g/4oz red rice miso
2 tsp sesame oil
2 tbs mirin
2 tbs soy sauce
6 spring onions, chopped

• Cook and drain the noodles according to instructions on the packet and reserve.
• Heat the dashi in a large pan, add the daikon, carrot, burdock root and pork and simmer for 20 minutes, skimming off any scum that appears on the surface.
• Add the miso to the hot soup and stir it in thoroughly, then add the sesame oil, mirin, soy sauce and spring onions. Serve with a portion of noodles in each bowl.

SERVES 4-6 [D][L]

CHICKEN WITH DEEP-FRIED RICE BALLS

Fun to make and fun to eat, this soup is a complete and very healthy meal in itself.

THE FRIED CHICKEN

2 chicken breasts, cut into strips

1 tbs mirin

1 tbs soy sauce

50g/2oz plain flour

1 tbs sesame seeds

Mixed vegetable and sesame oils

THE RICE BALLS

600g/1¼lb cooked white rice

5 spring onions, finely chopped

1 tbs sesame oil

2 tbs red rice miso

2 cloves garlic, chopped

2 tsp finely chopped root ginger

50g/2oz plain flour

50g/2oz sesame seeds

THE BROTH

1.25 litres/2 pints Chicken Stock

2 medium carrots, cut into thin strips

150g/5oz baby corn, cut into thin strips

150g/5oz Chinese cabbage, shredded

2 tbs chopped root ginger

2 tbs mirin

2 tbs soy sauce

150g/5oz beansprouts

4 spring onions, chopped

• Sprinkle the chicken with the mirin and soy sauce, turn to coat well and leave to marinate for 1 hour. Mix the flour and sesame seeds in a shallow dish, add the chicken strips and again turn to coat well. Heat the oils in a deep fryer and deep-fry the chicken until golden brown. Remove with a slotted spoon and drain on kitchen paper. Keep warm in a low oven.
• Combine all the ingredients for the rice balls in a bowl, apart from the flour and sesame seeds. Wet your fingers and roll the mixture into small balls. Mix the flour and sesame seeds in a shallow dish, add the balls and turn to coat well. Deep-fry the balls until brown in the oil used for the chicken. Remove and drain on kitchen paper, then keep warm in the oven.
• Heat up the chicken stock in a large pan and add all the ingredients apart from the beansprouts and spring onions. Simmer for 15 minutes. Finish the soup by adding the beansprouts and spring onions, and top off with the rice balls and chicken.
SERVES 4-6 [D][L]

SPRING MISO

The making of miso in Japan is a highly traditional process, with some recipes having been passed down through the family for centuries. Miso is a mixture of *koji* (cultured grain) and soya beans, left to ferment for anything from 6 weeks (for sweet misos) to 3 years (for dark, salty misos). We use a one-year-old brown rice miso paste to produce this rich-tasting, highly seasonal soup.

1.25 litres/2 pints Vegetable Stock or Dashi (see pages 147 and 150)

125g/4oz brown rice miso

2 tbs tamari (light soy sauce)

2 tsp chopped root ginger

125g/4oz carrot, diced

200g/7oz daikon, diced

200g/7oz watercress

200g/7oz spinach

6 spring onions, chopped

• Heat up the stock in a large pan, add the miso, tamari, ginger, carrot and daikon and simmer for 2–3 minutes.
• Add the watercress, spinach and chopped spring onions, cook for 2–3 more minutes and serve.
SERVES 4-6 [V][L][D][G]

BUCKWHEAT NOODLES WITH PRAWNS

Buckwheat or soba noodles are typically 20 per cent wheat and 80 per cent buckwheat. Their readiness to accept flavours makes them perfect for soup.

200g/7oz dried soba
   noodles
1 tablespoon sesame oil
12 large raw prawns,
   peeled and deveined,
   tail on
1 tsp sesame seeds
2 tbs tamari (light soy
   sauce)
1.25 litres/2 pints Light
   Dashi (see page 150)
2 tbs mirin
Pinch of salt
2 tsp root ginger, chopped
200g/7oz broccoli florets
4 spring onions, chopped

• Cook the noodles according to the instructions on the packet, refresh in cold water and reserve.
• Heat the sesame oil in a frying pan, add the prawns, sesame seeds and a dash of tamari, the mirin, salt and ginger. Add the broccoli, reserved prawns and spring onions and simmer for 2 minutes.
• To serve, pour the soup over a bed of noodles in each bowl.
SERVES 4 [D] [L]

MISO SOUP WITH BUTTERNUT SQUASH AND BUTTERBEANS

This is a rich yet mild winter soup which incorporates baked butternut squash and creamy butterbeans. If you add rice or noodles, you can turn it into a one-bowl meal.

150g/5oz butterbeans
1 medium butternut
   squash, peeled and
   seeded
1 tbs sesame oil
1 tbs vegetable oil
2 tsp sesame seeds
800ml/1³/4 pints Light
   Dashi (see page 150)
A small cube of ginger,
   sliced
4 fresh shiitake
   mushrooms, thinly
   sliced
3 level tbs red miso
A small bunch of spring
   onions, sliced
A drop or two of tamari
   to taste

• Soak the butterbeans overnight, then simmer in water for 1¹/2 hours or until soft and creamy. Reserve.
• Cut the squash into rough chunks and coat with the sesame and vegetable oils and the sesame seeds. Bake at 200°C/400°F/gas 6 for 25 minutes or until soft. Reserve.
• Heat up the dashi, then add the ginger, shiitake mushrooms and miso. Simmer for 5 minutes.
• Add the butternut squash, butterbeans and tamari and simmer for 5 more minutes.
• Add the spring onions and serve.
SERVES 4 [V] [G] [L]

CHANKO-NABE (SUMO WRESTLERS' STEW)

1 medium chicken, boned
   and cut into 5cm/2in
   chunks, bones reserved
2-3 leeks, sliced into
   rounds
4 carrots, cut into chunks
1 daikon or mooli (giant
   white radish, widely
   available in Asian
   supermarkets), shaved
   lengthwise and cut into
   fine shreds
1 large potato, cut into
   chunks
Salt
1-2 cakes deep-fried or
   plain tofu, cubed
10-12 shiitake mushrooms
   (pre-soaked if dried),
   sliced
2 medium onions,
   quartered
1 savoy cabbage, shredded
8 baby corns, cut into
   1cm/1/2in chunks
150ml/1/4 pint soy sauce
125ml/4fl oz mirin (or
   sherry or sake
   sweetened with sugar if
   unavailable)

If you are alarmed at the prospect of eating the food responsible for fattening up Japan's celebrated Sumo wrestlers, we should make it clear that it is the quantity of Chanko-Nabe they ingest, rather than the ingredients themselves, that is responsible for their prodigious size. That and the copious quantities of rice, beer and sake that they wash it all down with, together with the mandatory post-meal naps designed to maximize the conversion of calories into flesh. On its own, this stew is actually notably unfattening. It is also delicious enough to have spawned several dedicated Chanko restaurants serving variations on the basic theme in the Sumo-dominated Ryogoku district of Tokyo.

Sumo wrestlers live together in communal 'stables', and organize themselves into almost feudal heirarchies. It usually falls to the most junior wrestlers to prepare the vast metal pots of Chanko that form the everyday diet of the wrestlers, although some stables have a jealously guarded professional cook. The basic recipe is very flexible, and the chicken in the version below might easily be replaced by white fish or squid. The only serious Chanko taboo is the use of four-footed animals. Landing on all fours constitutes a loss in sumo, so the consumption of quadrupeds would be seen as a very bad omen prior to a bout.

• Put the chicken bones, leeks and carrots into a large pan of water and bring to the boil. Simmer for 3 hours, then strain. Parboil the daikon and potato in lightly salted water, then drain.
• Put the chicken meat, tofu, mushrooms, onions, cabbage, corn and strained stock into a large pan and add the soy sauce. Simmer until the chicken and the vegetables are cooked, then add the daikon and potato with the mirin and 1/2 teaspoon salt. Cook for a few more minutes, and serve steaming hot. Sumo wrestlers sometimes add fat white udon noodles to their Chanko.
SERVES 4 [D][L]

North America

FUSION COOKING may be all the rage at the moment, but in the USA it has been going on for centuries. The process which began with the first Spanish settlers finding a cornucopia of new goodies on their hands – corn, beans, chillies, potatoes and tomatoes – is still going strong today, as people of every culture arrive to grab their piece of the American Dream. In the intervening period, the melting pot has been enriched immeasurably by successive waves of Puritans, African slaves, East European Jews and all manner of pioneers and asylum seekers. One of the results has been the creation of some of the world's truly great soups.

Despite the avant-garde goings-on in America's trendiest restaurants, many of the recipes featured in this chapter have something distinctly old-fashioned and homely about them. The first European settlers were inevitably pioneers and usually Puritans, and neither category has much time for frills. Instead, they and their descendants produced soups with all the simplicity, solidity and wholesomeness of Shaker furniture. But the Pilgrim Fathers were a practical lot, and they readily incorporated indigenous ingredients into their diet, hence the presence of pumpkins, cranberries and turkey in the recipes that follow.

Not that the soups of America lack glamour. Chowders and gumbos have an allure enhanced by a million literary and movie references, and the soups of the Deep South in particular can be wildly hedonistic. It isn't difficult to imagine Rhett and Scarlett, or Elvis for that matter, tucking into a bowl or two of Crawfish, Black-Eyed Bean and Soft-Shell Crab Soup. France (particularly around New Orleans), Mexico, and above all Africa, via the slave trade, have contributed much exoticism to Southern soups. Gumbo, for instance, is a direct descendant of the okra-based stews of West Africa.

If you want proof of the American love of soup, just take a random walk through Manhattan. Soup bars are springing up on every corner. The Big Apple sometimes seems to be on the verge of transforming itself into the Big Ladle.

NEW ENGLAND CLAM CHOWDER

1.5kg/3lb fresh clams, or
 375g/12oz frozen clam
 meat
1 litre/1¾ pints Fish Stock
 (see page 147)
175g/6oz bacon or pork
 belly, diced
50g/2oz butter
300g/10oz onion, chopped
2 cloves garlic, chopped
500g/1lb potatoes, cut into
 1cm/½in cubes
50g/2oz crushed crackers
 or plain flour
175ml/6fl oz white wine
1–2 allspice berries
2 bay leaves
1 sprig of thyme
Salt and white pepper
300ml/½ pint double
 cream
3 corn-on-the-cobs, cooked
 and kernels shaved off
Flat-leaf parsley leaves, to
 garnish

In Moby Dick (published in 1851), the hero and his South Sea Islander harpoonist sidekick visit a Nantucket restaurant called the Try Pots. 'Clam or Cod?' asks the proprietress, succinctly. The pair choose clam, and then start worrying about how one bi-valve is possibly going to sustain them both. 'But when that smoking chowder came in, the mystery was delightfully explained. Oh sweet friends! Hearken to me. It was made of small juicy clams, scarcely bigger than hazelnuts, mixed with pounded ship biscuit, and salted pork cut into little flakes; the whole enriched with butter, and plentifully seasoned with pepper and salt . . . being surpassingly excellent, we despatched it with great expedition'.

Things haven't changed that much since 1851. Americans still down cups of clam chowder in their millions on both seaboards, and a good deal in between. Various versions exist – there is a heretical variety called Manhattan chowder which incorporates tomatoes and leaves out the cream – but all contain diced potato and salt pork or bacon as an absolute minimum. Of course, ship's biscuit isn't the force it was in Captain Ahab's day, but crushed crackers or plain old flour perform the same thickening function admirably.

The one drawback to chowder making this side of the pond comes in the clam department. Americans have the benefit of enormous, juicy, native quahog clams, which are unavailable in Europe except as frozen imports. However, our smaller (and sometimes grittier) Northern European clams make a very good substitute. Always use fresh clams if you can get hold of them – the juices they give off improve the flavour immeasurably.

- If you are using fresh clams, simmer them in the fish stock for 5 minutes, then strain the stock through muslin and reserve. Discard any shells which have failed to open, and remove the meat from the rest. If you are using one of the larger varieties of clams, chop them, otherwise leave them whole. If you are using frozen clam meat, defrost in advance.
- Dry-fry the bacon or pork belly in a large, heavy pan until nicely browned, then add the butter, onion and garlic and fry until soft. Meanwhile, heat up the stock to simmering point, and boil the potatoes in salted water for 10 minutes in a separate pan, until cooked. Mix the crackers or flour into the bacon mixture with a wooden spoon, then whisk in the hot stock and the wine. Add the allspice, bay leaves, thyme, salt and pepper. Simmer for a few minutes, then remove the bay leaves and thyme. Add the clams, potatoes, cream and corn. Simmer for a few more minutes and the chowder is ready to serve, garnished with parsley leaves.

SERVES 4-6

CRAWFISH, BLACK-EYED BEAN AND SOFT-SHELL CRAB SOUP

2 tbs olive oil

50g/1oz plain flour

50g/1oz butter

150g/5oz leek, chopped

250g/8oz onion, chopped

150g/5oz celery, chopped

1 tsp chopped garlic

1/2 tsp chilli powder

1 tsp paprika

250g/8oz red pepper,
   deseeded and chopped

150g/5oz bacon, chopped

1 litre/1 3/4 pints Chicken
   Stock (see page 147)

300ml/1/2 pint passata

250g/8oz black-eyed
   beans, soaked overnight
   and drained

2 bay leaves

1 sprig of thyme

1/2 tsp ground nutmeg

1/2 tsp ground cinnamon

4 cloves

10 live crawfish, or frozen
   tails

4–6 soft-shell crabs, live or
   frozen

Flour seasoned with
   paprika and salt,
   to coat the crabs

Vegetable oil

Paprika

Flat-leaf parsley, to
   garnish

We call them crayfish, Americans call them crawfish, but on either side of the Atlantic they are lively little beasts with the sweetest of flesh. Soft-shell crabs meanwhile are essentially regular crabs which have recently shed their shells to give themselves room to grow. This makes them extremely vulnerable to sea birds and hungry Americans from the Deep South. If you can find them fresh, rejoice, otherwise you'll need to make do with frozen ones. You won't mind – this is the last word in hedonism.

• Combine the olive oil and the flour in a heavy-bottomed pan and cook slowly for half an hour, stirring gently with a wooden spoon. Reserve the resulting roux, which should be nutty brown.

• Melt the butter in a large pan. Add the leek, onion, celery and garlic and fry gently until softened with the chilli powder, paprika, red peppers and bacon. Meanwhile, heat up the stock in a separate pan. Mix the passata and stock into the vegetables. Whisk in the roux, then stir in the black-eyed beans, bay leaves, thyme, nutmeg, cinnamon and cloves. Simmer for 1–1 1/2 hours, until the beans are soft. Towards the end, stir in the crawfish.

• Coat the soft-shell crabs in the seasoned flour. Fry them in vegetable oil and lay on top of the soup just before serving. Sprinkle with paprika and garnish with flat-leaf parsley.

SERVES 4-6

MICHIGAN MOREL SOUP

May is the month for morels in Michigan, and addicts flock in for the rich pickings. The morel is a sponge-headed mushroom, camouflaged to near invisibility, that grows where you least expect it, Michigan excepted. Dried, they sell for up to £300 per kg (£135 per lb). You can sometimes find fresh ones in specialist delicatessens, but nothing beats finding them yourself. In the UK, East Anglia is a good place to start foraging.

25g/1oz unsalted
    butter
375g/12oz fresh
    morels, the smaller
    the better, chopped,
    plus a few left
    whole, to garnish
Salt and freshly
    ground black pepper
1 litre/1¾ pints
    Chicken Stock (see
    page 147)
4 egg yolks
350ml/12fl oz double
    cream

• Melt the butter in a large, heavy pan, add the chopped and whole morels and fry them gently with a little salt and pepper. Add the stock and bring to the boil, then reduce to a simmer for a couple of minutes. Remove the whole morels and reserve.
• Whisk the egg yolks and the cream together, and slowly add the mixture to the morels. Make absolutely sure the mixture doesn't boil, or the soup will curdle and you'll be back in the wilderness searching for replacement mushrooms. Season to taste, garnish with the whole morels, and consider yourself privileged.
SERVES 4-6 [G]

CHILLI BEEF SOUP

The ubiquitous *chilli con carne* originated in Mexico, ending up on school menus everywhere completely drained of character. Only a lucky break with a Mormon missionary and a traditional family recipe in Albuquerque restored Nick to the faith. New Mexico, as far as he's concerned, is now the chilli beef capital of the world.

250g/8oz minced beef
220g/7¼oz onion,
    finely chopped
30ml olive oil
15g red chilli,
    approx. 1tsp finely
    chopped
1 heaped tsp ground
    cumin
1 heaped tspn paprika
2 cloves garlic, finely
    chopped
A pinch of cayenne
    pepper
20g balsamic vinegar,
    approx. 1 tbs
750 ml/1¼fl oz
    chicken stock (see
    page 147)
350g/1½oz chopped
    tomatoes
3 fresh bay leaves
400g/13oz kidney
    beans, canned or
    dried
Juice of 1 lime
Salt to taste

• If you are planning to use dried kidney beans, you'll need to soak them overnight. You'll want about 180g/6¼oz dry weight.
• Using a large thick-bottomed saucepan over a medium flame, fry the minced beef, chopped onion, olive oil, red pepper, red chilli, cumin, paprika, garlic, cayenne and balsamic vinegar together for at least 15 minutes until the onion has softened. Make sure you break up the mince thoroughly.
• Add half the kidney beans to the chicken stock and blend until smooth.
• Add the blended chicken stock to the mince mixture, together with the tomato purée, chopped tomatoes and bay leaf.
• Simmer for at least an hour. The longer you cook it, the better it will become.
• Finally, add the rest of the kidney beans, the lime juice and salt.
• This soup is excellent with any or all of the following: rice, soft tortillas, sour cream and grated cheddar.
SERVES 4-6 [G]

CHICKEN, BLACK-EYED BEAN AND BACON GUMBO

There are many varieties of gumbo, the quintessential stew of the Deep South, but what unites them all is a heavy reliance on okra. Originally brought to the region from its native Africa during the slavery era, okra is the only vegetable member of a family of plants which has had other striking successes in the Southern USA, notably with cotton and the kola nut (the latter being a key ingredient in a certain black fizzy drink from Atlanta). It has a distinctive, silky texture (some would even call it slimy) which makes it a thickening agent in its own right, and it works wonders in the savoury recipe that follows.

• Drain the black-eyed beans then boil them in salted water for about 1½ hours until soft. Drain and reserve.
• Mix 25g/1oz flour, a little of the paprika and salt and pepper on a plate and use to coat the chicken pieces. Heat 1 tablespoon of the olive oil in a large, heavy-bottomed pan, add the chicken and brown for 10 minutes. Remove from the pan and reserve. Brown the bacon in the same pan for a few minutes, remove with a slotted spoon and reserve.
• Scrape up the bits off the surface of the pan, but leave them in to flavour the finished product. Add 1–2 tablespoons of olive oil and then the remaining flour, stirring to form a thick paste. Turn the heat low and cook the paste for about 30 minutes, stirring continuously to prevent it burning. Eventually it will turn into a nutty brown roux. Meanwhile, heat up the stock in a separate pan.
• Remove the roux from the pan and pour in the remaining olive oil over medium heat. Add the onion, peppers, garlic and tabasco, cover and sweat for 5 minutes, then return the roux and stir it in with the tomato purée, cloves, cinnamon, nutmeg and cumin. Gradually whisk in the stock together with the passata.
• Add the okra and simmer for 10 minutes. Now add the black-eyed beans, the chicken, bacon and the fresh herbs, season to taste, and simmer for another 10 minutes. Serve with steaming hot long-grain rice.
SERVES 6-8 [D]

250g/8oz black-eyed beans, soaked overnight
Salt and freshly ground black pepper
75g/3oz plain flour
1 tsp paprika
425g/14oz chicken fillet, chopped into 2.5cm/1in cubes
75ml/3fl oz olive oil
150g/5oz streaky bacon, chopped
1.5 litres/2½ pints Chicken Stock (see page 147)
150g/5oz onion, chopped
2 red peppers, chopped, cored and deseeded
2 green peppers, chopped, cored and deseeded
1 tsp chopped garlic
1-2 tsp tabasco sauce
4 cloves
¼ tsp ground cinnamon
¼ tsp ground nutmeg
1 tsp toasted cumin seeds
2 tbs tomato purée
200ml/7fl oz passata
200g/7oz okra, sliced diagonally
1 bunch chopped parsley
1 bunch chopped oregano
2 sprigs of thyme
4 bay leaves

PUMPKIN AND CRANBERRY SOUP

The typical American has to get through a fair amount of pumpkin and cranberries during the latter part of the year. Something must be done with the innards of all those Jack-o'-lanterns at Halloween, pumpkin pie is a vital part of Thanksgiving, and those Thanksgiving and Christmas turkeys just wouldn't be the same without that juicy cranberry sauce. It is just as well, then, that this rather good soup has evolved to deal with the excess.

THE SAUCE
425g/14oz fresh
    cranberries
200ml/7fl oz water
150g/5oz sugar
THE SOUP
75ml/3fl oz olive oil
125g/4oz celery,
    chopped
125g/4oz leek,
    chopped
1/2 tsp cayenne pepper
600g/1lb 4oz pumpkin
    flesh, chopped into
    2.5cm/1in cubes
1 tbs chopped fresh
    sage
1.25 litres/2 pints
    Chicken or
    Vegetable Stock
    (see page 147)
Salt and white pepper
125ml/4fl oz double
    cream

• To make the sauce, boil the cranberries in the water until they have disintegrated. Add the sugar, and continue boiling until it has dissolved. Now blend the mixture in a food processor and reserve. If there is any left over after you have eaten the soup, you can use it as regular cranberry sauce.
• To make the soup, begin by heating the olive oil in a large pan. Add the leek, celery and cayenne, cover and sweat for 5 minutes, then add the pumpkin cubes and the sage and cook over medium heat, stirring frequently, until the pumpkin is soft.
• Pour in the stock, simmer for 5 minutes, then blend in a food processor. Adjust the seasoning, whisk in the double cream and serve, with the cranberry sauce either piped on the surface in intriguing patterns or dolloped on more prosaically.
SERVES 4-6 [G][OPTIONALLY V]

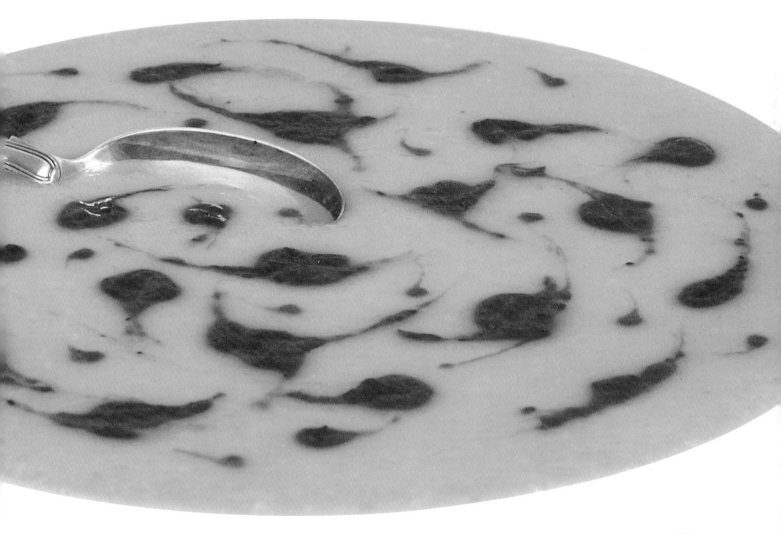

BROCCOLI AND SWEETCORN CHOWDER

We couldn't take this item off the SOUP works menu for long for fear of provoking local uprisings. The broccoli and sweetcorn provide the crunch, the tarragon-infused cream the velvety backdrop.

50g/2oz butter
125g/4oz carrot, sliced
125g/4oz leek, sliced
125g/4oz celery, sliced
125g/4oz onion, sliced
50g/2oz plain flour
1.25 litres/2 pints
   Vegetable Stock
   (see page 147)
600g/1¼lb broccoli,
   chopped, florets and
   stalks kept separate
Salt and white pepper
6 corn-on-the-cobs,
   kernels shaved off
1 tbs chopped tarragon
1 tbs chopped parsley
200ml/7fl oz cream

• Melt the butter in a large pan over moderate heat, add the carrot, leek, celery and onion, cover and sweat for 5–10 minutes, until soft. Add the flour and stir it in until well incorporated. Meanwhile, heat up the stock in a separate pan.
• Whisk in the vegetable stock, then add the broccoli stalks and a little white pepper. Bring to the boil, reduce to a simmer for 10 minutes, then blend in a food processor.
• Return the soup to the pan over heat, add the corn and the broccoli florets and simmer for 5–10 minutes. Finally, add the herbs and cream and a little salt to taste, bring up to temperature and serve.
SERVES 4-6 [v]

TOMATO, BLUE CHEESE AND BACON

The pungent creaminess of a blue cheese such as Gorgonzola or Stilton complements the crunchy bacon particularly well in this simple and satisfying recipe.

8 tomatoes
1 tbs olive oil
200g/7oz streaky
   bacon
50g/2oz butter
150g/5oz onion, sliced
125g/4oz celery, sliced
125g/4oz carrot, sliced
1.25 litres/2 pints
   Chicken Stock (see
   page 147)
50g/2oz plain flour
300g/10oz blue
   cheese, crumbled
150ml/5fl oz double
   cream
Salt and freshly
   ground black pepper
4 spring onions,
   chopped
1 tbs chopped flat-leaf
   parsley

• Preheat the oven to 220°C/425°F/gas 7. Place the tomatoes in a roasting tin and sprinkle with the olive oil. Roast for 30 minutes, then blend in a food processor and reserve.
• Grill the streaky bacon quite slowly until evenly browned and crispy, making sure you reserve the fat. Crumble the cooked bacon into smallish pieces and reserve.
• Pour the bacon fat into a large pan over moderate heat, add the butter and sweat the onion, carrot and celery for 5 minutes, covered. Meanwhile, heat up the stock in a separate pan. Add the flour and stir until absorbed. Pour in the chicken stock with the cheese and the puréed tomatoes, bring to the boil briefly, then blend in a food processor. Return to the pan to warm through, add the cream and season to taste. Serve with the bacon, spring onions and parsley sprinkled on top and a hunk of sourdough bread on the side.
SERVES 4-6

SMOKED TURKEY LENTIL

8 tomatoes
3 tbs olive oil
250g/8oz smoked turkey
    fillet, cubed
¼ tsp mustard powder
1 tsp paprika
Salt and freshly ground
    black pepper
1 tsp cumin seeds
125g/4oz celery, chopped
200g/7oz onion, chopped
1 red pepper, cored,
    deseeded and diced
1 yellow pepper, cored,
    deseeded and diced
4 chipotle chillies, soaked,
    deseeded and chopped
4 cloves garlic, chopped
½ tsp ground allspice
250g/8oz green lentils
2 bay leaves
1 glass red wine
1.25 litres/2 pints Chicken
    Stock (see page 147)
1 tbs chopped oregano
1 tbs chopped parsley
1 sprig of thyme

The American love affair with the turkey goes back to the Pilgrim Fathers and long before. In this recipe, the smoked variety is combined with smoky chipotle chillies to produce a spicy and addictive soup which is, well, smoky.

• Preheat the oven to 220°C/425°F/gas 7. Place the tomatoes in a roasting tin and sprinkle with a little olive oil. Roast them for 30 minutes, then blend in a food processor and reserve.
• Heat half the oil in a large, heavy pan. Coat the smoked turkey in the mustard powder, half the paprika and a little salt and black pepper and fry in the oil until brown. Remove with a slotted spoon and reserve.
• Add the remaining olive oil and fry the cumin seeds for 2–3 minutes until they give off a nutty smell. Then add the celery, onion, peppers, chillies, garlic, allspice and the rest of the paprika and fry gently until the vegetables are soft.
• Add the puréed tomatoes, the lentils, bay leaves, wine and stock and bring to the boil. Reduce the heat, cover and simmer until the lentils are soft, adding more stock or water if necessary. Finally, add the herbs and season to taste. Serve with the smoked turkey cubes sprinkled on top of the soup.
SERVES 4-6 [G][D]

Central and South America

THE SOUPS and stews of the Americas south of the Rio Grande are probably as little known to the majority of Westerners as anything in this book. This is either a pity or a glorious opportunity depending on how you look at it. Latin-American soups and stews are a revelation. Filled with life, they are the natural products of a corner of the globe that really knows how to party.

As one local food writer would have it, for Latin Americans soup is as predictable as the sunrise. Yet prior to the arrival of the conquistadors in the sixteenth century, the indigenous population scarcely bothered with it at all. It didn't take long, however, for the inexorable processes of cross-fertilization to begin. The Spanish settlers soon found themselves supplementing the chickpeas, white beans, cabbage and parsnips which formed the basis of their favourite soups with exotic local vegetables like the yucca and calabash. The coming of the Portuguese with their love of thick cozido stews further sweetened the pot, and the mix was completed with the arrival of slaves from Africa.

The typical ingredients of Latin-American soups and stews vary considerably from country to country. Mexicans favour beans, strips of corn tortilla and the gamut of chillies from the benign to the sizzling (the Mayan name for the habañero, the fiercest of the lot, translates as 'the crying tongue', which aptly captures both what it does and what it looks like). Columbians and the people of the Andes are the potato experts and are quite capable of using three different varieties in the same soup – one to melt into the broth, one to keep its shape and yet another to provide colour and flavour. Brazil is the most obviously African influenced nation, with palm oil, coconut milk and peppered shrimps complementing indigenous ingredients such as manioc (cassava) flour. Chile looks like one big beach on the map, and duly provides wonderful seafood soups, called 'mating soups' by the locals in tribute to their supposed aphrodisiac effects. Finally, we come to Uruguay and Argentina, where the one thing you can count on is beef.

What unites the soups of all these countries is more about how they are cooked and eaten than what goes in them. One-pot cooking is king, and tends to be carried out so slowly that the usual distinctions between soup, stew and porridge collapse in the melding of flavours. Above all, the cooking of a soup is seen as a reason to throw a party. All across the continent, friends and families gather together on a Sunday to take pot luck. Put on some salsa music, head to the stove, and find out at first hand what draws them there.

SOUR CEVICHE

375g/12oz sushi quality
   tuna, thinly sliced
Juice of 3 limes
1.25 litres/2 pints Fish
   Stock (see page 149)
250g/8oz red onion, finely
   chopped
3 spring onions, chopped
1 tbs chopped oregano
2 roasted red peppers,
   skinned, cored,
   deseeded and chopped
4 plum tomatoes, skinned,
   deseeded and chopped
2 red chillies, deseeded
   and chopped
1 tbs chopped flat-leaf
   parsley
50g/2oz black olives,
   stoned and chopped
4 cloves garlic, chopped
250g/8oz courgettes,
   boiled whole for
   5 minutes, then sliced
Salt and freshly ground
   black pepper
250ml/8fl oz sour cream,
   to garnish

As this soup goes to prove, the Japanese are a long way from having a monopoly on the consumption of raw fish. Mexicans adore it marinaded, in the dish they call ceviche. Though not usually served in soup form, ceviche adapts particularly well to the presence of a spicy, chilled stock. The tuna used in the recipe must be top quality and so fresh it is virtually odourless. If you eat oysters and/or smoked salmon but are horrified by the thought of raw fish, you don't really have a leg to stand on.

• Lay the fish in a shallow dish, pour on the lime juice, turn to coat and leave to marinate for half an hour. Combine the rest of the ingredients in a serving bowl, with the exception of the sour cream.
• Add the fish to the bowl, and chill until ready to serve, garnished with sour cream.
SERVES 4 [L][D]

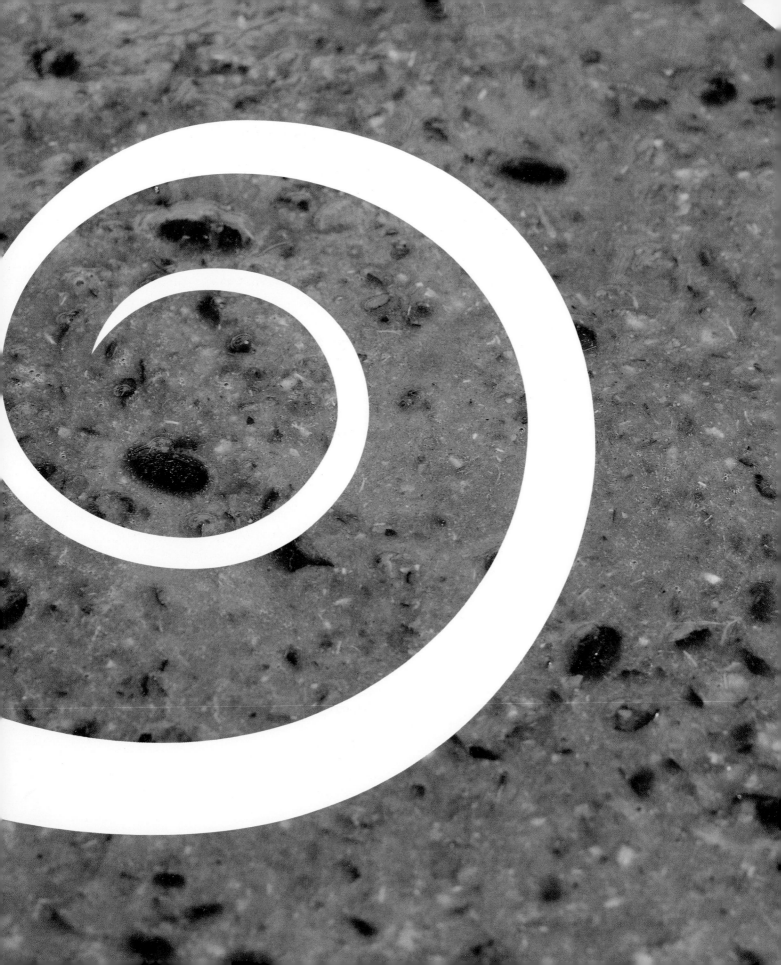

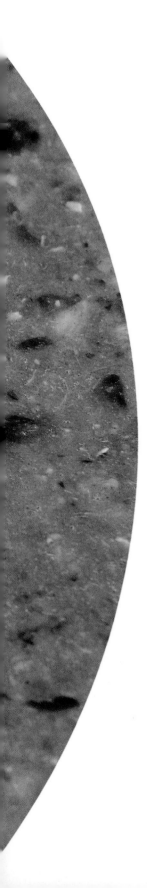

MEXICAN BLACK BEAN

Nick was on a catered fishing holiday in the Yucatan peninsula a few years ago. One afternoon, he visited a local market and then snuck into the kitchen to indulge his secret passion for soup-making. When the matriarchal caterer found he was making black-bean soup, she lost all respect for him, believing it to be peasant food beneath her dignity. More fool her. The beans in question are sweet and wonderful in soups, and the sepia colour they give to this one is a reason for making it in itself.

2 tbs olive oil

200g/7oz shallots,
    finely chopped

4 cloves garlic,
    chopped

2 red or green chillies,
    deseeded and
    chopped

6 tomatoes, skinned
    and chopped

2 litres/3½ pints
    Vegetable or
    Chicken Stock (see
    page 147)

250g/8oz black beans,
    soaked overnight
    and drained

Salt and freshly
    ground black pepper

1 small bunch
    coriander, chopped

Juice of 2 limes

200g/7oz grated
    cheese, to garnish

Pinch each of ground
    cinnamon and
    nutmeg, to garnish

• Heat the oil in a large, heavy pan. Add the shallots, garlic and chillies and fry until they have softened, then add the chopped tomatoes and fry for 2–3 minutes longer. Add the stock and beans and bring to the boil. Reduce to a slow simmer, cover and cook for about 2 hours, or until the beans are soft.

• Blend the soup to a purée in a food processor, and season to taste. Stir in the coriander and lime juice and serve garnished with grated cheese and a pinch of cinnamon and nutmeg.

SERVES 4-6   [G][OPTIONALLY V]

SOUP

TOMATILLO

The tomatillo, or Mexican tomato, is a close relative of the cape gooseberry, for all you botanists out there. It is harvested when still green, and comes encased in a papery husk or calyx which must be removed before cooking. Raw, it is an essential constituent of an authentic guacamole, but cooking brings out its flavour, which is rather like that of a tart apple. Tomatillos are increasingly available in funkier supermarkets, and this spicy recipe gives them a chance to show off their distinctive qualities.

125ml/4fl oz olive oil
125g/4oz white onion, chopped
4 cloves garlic, chopped
3 hot red chillies, deseeded and chopped
1 tsp cumin seeds, dry-toasted in a frying pan
1 kg/2lb tomatillos, husks removed, roughly chopped
1.25 litres/2 pints Chicken or Vegetable Stock
Salt and freshly ground black pepper
1 tbs chopped oregano, chopped
1 tbs chopped parsley, chopped

GARNISH
150g/5oz streaky bacon, grilled slowly until crisp
50g/2oz red onion, chopped

• Heat the olive oil in a large pan, add the onion, garlic, chillies and cumin, cover and sweat over moderate heat for 2–3 minutes. Add the tomatillos and cook for 5 minutes. Meanwhile, heat up the stock in a separate pan.
• Add the stock to the vegetables, bring to the boil, then simmer for 10 minutes. Remove from the heat and pass through a mouli or blend thoroughly in a food processor. Return to the heat, season with salt and pepper and add the oregano and parsley.
• Serve with the grilled bacon crumbled on top and a garnish of chopped red onion.
SERVES 6 [L][D][G]

SHRIMP TORTILLA WITH SOUR CREAM

This is a fairly complicated soup to prepare, but given a special occasion it is well worth the effort. The tortillas in question are the soft variety (which at other times you might find wrapped around your enchilada) rather than the hard corn taco type.

12 large raw prawns, peeled and deveined, tails on, heads and shells reserved
12 large mild red chillies, deseeded and left whole
3 cloves garlic, chopped
Salt and freshly ground black pepper
1/2 tsp paprika
Juice of 2 limes
4 red peppers
2 chipotle chillies
1 litre/1 3/4 pints Fish Stock (see page 149)
4 soft tortillas, toasted and cut into thirds
200g/7oz onions, sliced
125g/4oz carrots, chopped
75ml/3fl oz olive oil
6 tomatoes, deseeded and chopped
1 small bunch coriander, roughly chopped
1 small bunch flat-leaf parsley, roughly chopped
1 small bunch oregano, roughly chopped
1 small bunch mint, roughly chopped
1 sprig of thyme
200g/7oz canned chickpeas
125ml/4fl oz sour cream, to garnish (optional)

• Place the prawns in a bowl with the red chillies, half the garlic, a little salt and pepper, the paprika and half the lime juice, turn to coat and leave to marinate for 1 hour. Thread the prawns and chillies on to presoaked kebab sticks and remove to the fridge.

• Meanwhile, preheat the oven to 230°C/450°F/gas 8. Roast the red peppers according to the instructions on page 156. Skin, deseed and chop the peppers. Deseed the chipotles, roughly chop them and boil them for 10 minutes in just enough water to cover. Blend in a food processor and reserve.

• Heat the stock over moderate heat in a large pan. Add the prawn shells and heads, simmer for 10 minutes and strain, reserving the stock. Toast the soft tortillas in a griddle pan until slightly branded, cut into thirds and reserve.

• To make the soup, heat the olive oil in a large pan. Add the onions, carrots and remaining garlic and fry for 10 minutes over moderate heat until soft. Add the tomatoes and continue cooking for 5 minutes. Add the fish stock, chipotles, all the herbs, the chickpeas and most of the chopped and roasted red peppers, and simmer for 10 more minutes. Blend in a food processor and season to taste.

• Grill or barbecue the prawn kebabs for 2–3 minutes each side over or under moderate heat.

• Ladle the soup into bowls and garnish with the tortilla wedges, remaining red pepper, and sour cream, if using. Lay one prawn kebab across each bowl, sprinkle with the remaining lime juice and serve.

SERVES 4

CHILEAN SHRIMP AND SCALLOP

1.25 litres/2 pints Fish
  Stock (see page 149)
600g/1lb 4oz raw prawns,
  peeled and deveined,
  heads and shells
  reserved
200ml/7fl oz olive oil
200g/7oz onion, chopped
4 cloves garlic, chopped
3 jalapeño chillies
2 tsp paprika
10 tomatoes, skinned,
  deseeded and chopped
1 large sprig of thyme
2 bay leaves
1 small bunch oregano,
  chopped
425g/14oz new potatoes
Salt and freshly ground
  black pepper
425g/14oz shelled scallops
1 small bunch flat-leaf
  parsley, chopped
Juice of 2 lemons

With that much coastline, it would be surprising if Chile couldn't come up with some cracking seafood soups. This one, which was inspired by a recipe from *The Art of South American Cooking* by Myra Waldo, proves beyond all doubt that they can. If you can't find jalapeño chillies, any other hot green ones will do.

• Heat the stock in a large pan, add the prawn heads and shells and simmer for 15 minutes. Strain, reserving the stock.
• Heat 50ml/2fl oz of the oil in a large pan over moderate heat. Add the onion, garlic, chillies and ½ teaspoon of the paprika and fry for 10 minutes, stirring frequently. Add the tomatoes and stock with the thyme, bay leaves and oregano and simmer for 20 minutes.
• Meanwhile, slice the potatoes and sprinkle them with salt, pepper and a little of the remaining paprika. Heat 75ml/3fl oz of the olive oil in a frying pan and fry the potatoes over moderate heat until well browned, turning frequently. Remove and keep warm in a low oven (140°C/275°F/gas 1).
• Heat the remaining oil in a clean frying pan. Coat the scallops and prawns in the remaining paprika and a little salt and pepper and fry over quite a high heat. Do this in batches or they won't brown properly. Don't fry any individual piece of shellfish for more than 2–3 minutes. Throw the seafood into the soup, adjust the seasoning and simmer for 4–5 minutes.
• Serve topped with the browned potatoes, chopped parsley and a liberal squeeze of lemon juice.
SERVES 4-6 [D][L][G]

LENTIL CHILLI WITH CHIPOTLE

4-6 chipotle chillies,
depending on desired
potency
2 red peppers, roasted,
skinned, cored,
deseeded and chopped
6 tomatoes, roasted and
puréed
50g/2fl oz olive oil
150g/5oz streaky bacon,
diced
200g/7oz onions, sliced
3 cloves garlic, chopped
1 tsp cumin seeds, dry-
toasted in a frying pan
1.5 litres/2½ pints Chicken
or Duck and Pork Stock
(see pages 147 and 149)
1 tsp dried cep
(mushroom) powder or
25g/1oz dried porcini,
finely chopped
200g/7oz green lentils
4 cloves
Salt and freshly ground
black pepper
2 tbs lime juice
1 small bunch coriander,
chopped
Grated Cheddar, to garnish

The chipotle is a smoked, dried chilli originating from Mexico. Used sparingly in any dish, they impart an incredible hot, woody flavour. In this recipe, the chipotle has a particularly enlivening effect on the lentils. Chipotles must be handled with respect, and need to be soaked and deseeded before use.

• Soak the chillies for 1 hour in enough tepid water to cover, then drain, reserving the soaking water, deseed and thinly slice.
• Preheat the oven to 230°C/450°F/gas 8. Roast the peppers and tomatoes for 30 minutes in the oven. Then skin, core, deseed and chop the peppers and reserve. Purée the tomatoes and reserve.
• Heat the oil in a large pan and fry the bacon until lightly browned. Add the onions, garlic, chillies and cumin seeds and cook gently for about 5 minutes, until the vegetables have softened. Meanwhile, heat up the stock in a separate pan. Add the mushroom powder or dried mushrooms to the vegetables and mix thoroughly. Pour in the stock and the reserved soaking water and add the lentils, cloves and puréed tomatoes. Bring to the boil, then reduce the heat, cover and simmer for about 2 hours.
• Add the peppers and simmer for another 10 minutes. Season to taste and add the lime juice and chopped coriander. Serve topped with grated Cheddar, with hot, flat bread on the side.

SERVES 4-6 [G]

HOT SPICY CHICKEN WITH GUACAMOLE

425g/14oz chicken fillets, skinned and cut into wedges

2 scotch bonnet chillies, deseeded and finely chopped

3 cloves garlic, finely chopped

1/2 tsp ground cumin

Juice of 2 limes

Salt and freshly ground black pepper

75ml/3fl oz olive oil

150g/5oz white onion, chopped

1.25 litres/2 pints Chicken Stock (see page 147)

5 ripe, medium avocados, peeled, stoned and chopped

1 red pepper, deseeded, cored and chopped

5 tomatoes, skinned, deseeded and chopped

50g/2oz red onion, finely chopped

1 small bunch coriander, leaves only, chopped, reserving a few to garnish

1 green chilli, deseeded and chopped, to garnish

Guacamole, as everyone knows, makes an excellent dip. What fewer people know is that, with a little bit of magic, it can also be transformed into a mean soup. Ideally you should peel and stone the avocados just before use, to prevent browning. If you want to prepare them ahead of time, coat the flesh with lemon juice, wrap tightly in clingfilm and refrigerate until required.

• Place the chicken in a shallow dish with half the chillies and garlic, the cumin, a quarter of the lime juice and salt and black pepper. Turn to coat and leave to marinate for 2–3 hours.
• Brush a ridged grill pan with oil. Remove the chicken from the marinade and fry until well browned on both sides, about 10 minutes, turning frequently. Transfer the chicken to an oven dish and place in a low oven (140°C/275°F/gas 1) to keep warm.
• Pour the remaining oil into the pan, add the onion, remaining chillies and garlic and fry gently for about 5 minutes, or until soft. Pour in the chicken stock and remaining lime juice and add the avocados. Bring to the boil briefly, then remove from the heat and blend in a food processor.
• Return the soup to the pan on the heat, add the peppers, tomatoes, red onion, coriander and seasoning and simmer for 3–4 minutes.
• Serve with chicken wedges on each portion, together with a sprinkling of green chilli and a coriander sprig to garnish.
SERVES 4-6 [G][L]

VENEZUELAN CREAM OF CELERIAC

If you've ever wondered what they eat in Venezuela, here is part of the answer. Celeriac, called 'abune' by the locals, is like a more pungent and flavoursome version of celery. The rum in this recipe is strictly non-traditional, but it gives this tasty soup an extra lift. Douglas Rodriquez's *Latin Ladies* inspired us to action here.

75g/3oz butter
150g/5oz onion, sliced
4 cloves garlic, chopped
125g/4oz celery, roughly chopped
50g/2oz plain flour
1.25 litres/2 pints Chicken Stock (see page 147)
250g/8oz potato, peeled and roughly chopped
425g/14oz celeriac, peeled and roughly chopped
2 bay leaves
50ml/2fl oz dark rum
150ml/¼ pint double cream
Salt and white pepper
Grated cheese, to garnish

• Melt the butter in a large pan over moderate heat. Add the onion, garlic and celery and fry for 10 minutes, then turn the heat down low, add the flour and mix thoroughly with a wooden spoon until well incorporated.
• Stir in the stock and drop in the potato, celeriac and bay leaves. Simmer for 45 minutes, remove the bay leaves and blend in a food processor.
• Return to the pan, add the rum, double cream and salt and pepper to taste and bring to the boil briefly. Serve garnished with grated cheese.

SERVES 4-6

RED BEAN SOUP

The beans in question are the kidney variety familiar from chilli con carne. Variations on this soup are made all over Latin America, but this particular example hails from Colombia. The beans and the tender pork fillet make a lovely couple, in terms of texture as well as flavour.

3 tbs olive oil
1 tsp cumin seeds
150g/5oz onions, sliced
4 cloves garlic, chopped
50g/5oz bacon, diced
150g/5oz carrot, diced small
10 tomatoes, peeled and deseeded
2 litres/3½ pints Chicken Stock (see page 147)
425g/14oz pork fillet, cut into small dice
425g/14oz red kidney beans, soaked overnight and drained
2 green plantains, peeled and diced
1 sprig of thyme
2 bay leaves
1 small bunch coriander, chopped
2 tbs chopped oregano
salt and freshly ground black pepper

• Heat the oil in a large pan over a medium heat and fry the cumin seeds for just under a minute, until they start to turn brown. Add the onion, garlic, bacon and carrot, and fry for 10 minutes. Then drop in the tomatoes, and continue to fry for 2–3 more minutes.
• Pour in the stock and add the pork fillet, beans, plantain, thyme and bay leaves. Cover and simmer for 1½ hours, adding more stock if too much liquid evaporates.
• Add the coriander and oregano at the last minute, season to taste and serve.

SERVES 4-6 [D][G]

COZIDO (BRAZILIAN BEEF AND SAUSAGE STEW)

75ml/3fl oz olive oil

4 cloves garlic, chopped

200g/7oz red onion, sliced

1 tsp deseeded and
chopped red chilli,

1 tsp paprika

1 tsp cumin seeds

425g/14oz pork ribs, cut
into small sections

200g/7oz smoked streaky
bacon, chopped

250g/8oz Portuguese
sausage or chorizo, cut
into bite-sized chunks

500g/1lb chuck steak,
cubed

2 litres/3½ pints Beef
Stock (see page 148)

1 small bunch thyme

200g/7oz cabbage,
shredded

200g/7oz carrots, diced

425g/14oz pumpkin, diced

2 plantains, peeled and cut
into sections

4 corn-on-the-cobs,
kernels shaved off

425g/14oz sweet potato,
cut into large dice

200g/7oz okra, roughly
chopped

425g/14oz vegetable
marrow, roughly
chopped

Salt and freshly ground
black pepper

Juice of 4 limes

1 bunch flat-leaf parsley,
chopped, to garnish

In its native Portugal, cozido is a little like the Italian *bollito misto* or the French *pot au feu*, but its journey across the Atlantic has made for something altogether more exotic. In fact, we have had to temper the exoticism somewhat in the recipe that follows. In Brazil, cozido would typically be served with a marrow bone in each portion, something that until recently could have wound you up in court in the present BSE-phobic UK. It would also feature manioc flour on the side, for each diner to use to thicken their cozido to taste, and esoteric vegetables such as xuxu which our local supermarket was fresh out of last time we looked. Nevertheless, what remains produces a tremendous tropical party stew, and you needn't wait until Brazil next win the World Cup to enjoy it. Just make sure you have a vast pan to hand, or you'll never get it all in.

• Heat 50ml/2fl oz of the olive oil in a large pan. Add the garlic, red onion, chilli, paprika and cumin and fry over moderate heat for 10 minutes. Remove the vegetables and reserve. Add the remaining olive oil and fry all the meats in small batches until browned and sealed. Return the vegetables to the pan, reduce the heat, and cook for 10 minutes, turning frequently.
• Add the beef stock and thyme, cover and simmer for 1½ hours. You can skim off any fat that forms on the surface, but we don't as we like to keep it rustic and wholesome.
• Add all the vegetables and simmer for another 15 minutes. Season to taste and finish off with the lime juice and chopped parsley.
SERVES 10-12 [D]

Africa and the Caribbean

PERHAPS because there is relatively little indigenous restaurant culture in Africa, with the continent's cookery rooted firmly in the home, African soups and stews have not received the attention in the West that they deserve. With more than 300 million people and over 800 languages, Africa south of the Sahara is a mighty big place about which to generalise. There are, however, certain culinary themes which unite this vast continent, and all of them can be found in the region's delicious soups and stews.

African cooking comes straight from the heart. Rigid recipes are rare, and feel is everything. Soups come together in an almost organic process, full of rhythm and life. There are ingredients which crop up again and again in African cooking. Yam and sweet potato, plantain and cassava are all Pan-African staples. Special mention must be made of chillies, unknown in Africa prior to 1500, which took only 50 years to conquer the continent once they arrived from the New World. Another feature of the typical African diet is an emphasis on one-pot cooking. This is good news for the soup lover. Meat tends to be used sparingly as a flavouring, if at all, and soups and stews are usually served with starchy supplements such as ground rice, boiled yam or pounded maize.

The soups of the Caribbean betray African influences and many more besides. The Jamaica national motto, 'out of many, one people', perfectly captures the cultural diversity of the region. This, combined with the islands' lush climates and abundant seafood, has the happy by-product of a splendid range of nourishing soups. The original inhabitants, the Arawaks, have all but died out, but their legacy appears in words like 'barbecue', 'potato'

and 'guava', which give some clue to their diet. The Columbus regime brought bananas, citrus fruits and sugar cane to the islands from the Canaries to supplement the indigenous ingredients, and exotic crops like sweet potato and breadfruit arrived in the eighteenth century.

The culinary melting pot was further enhanced by the arrival of indentured labourers from India and China following the abolition of slavery in the nineteenth century, bringing new spices, flavours and cooking techniques. The colonial powers of France, Britain and the Netherlands have all left their mark but the most powerful influence on the food comes from West Africa, via the slave trade.

Health is of paramount importance to the people of the Caribbean. Locals, if offered a drink, will often choose a nutritious branded health supplement rather than a more traditional tipple. Naturally, this is all reflected in the region's soups and stews, from the wholesome Ital concoctions of the Rastafarians to the luxuriant delights of Trinidadian callaloo.

TRINIDADIAN CRAB SOUP

Johnny once stayed in a village in the Caribbean just next to a mangrove swamp where there were so many crabs you were more likely than not to nail one just by swinging a machete groundwards with your eyes shut. With such natural riches, it is not surprising that the region produces so many excellent crab dishes. The simple, vivacious soup that follows is an excellent example.

2 tbs olive oil
250g/8oz fresh crab meat, chopped
1/2 tsp salt
2 tsp chopped root ginger
125g/4oz shallots, finely chopped
1 tbs tomato purée
1.25 litres/2 pints Chicken Stock (see page 147)
2 eggs
1 tbs vinegar (not malt)
2 tbs medium sherry
2 spring onions, chopped

• Heat the oil in a large, heavy pan. Add the crab, salt, ginger and shallots and fry gently for 5 minutes. Add the tomato purée and stir it in. Meanwhile, heat up the stock in a separate pan.
• Stir in the stock and simmer very gently for 10 minutes. Meanwhile, beat together the eggs, vinegar and sherry, and add to the soup in a slow, steady stream. Add the spring onions and simmer for 5 more minutes, then serve.
SERVES 4-6 [D][L][G]

SHRIMP AND OKRA STEW

This full-tasting and tangy West African stew is the godfather of gumbo. Excellent party food (hence the beer), particularly if you cook the prawns on a barbecue.

1 tsp cumin seeds
16 medium raw tiger prawns, peeled
1 tsp paprika
Salt and freshly ground black pepper
4 cloves garlic, chopped
Juice of 2 limes
2 tbs olive oil
175g/6oz bacon or pork belly, diced
3 small red chillies, chopped and deseeded
250g/8oz shallots, chopped
8 medium tomatoes, skinned and deseeded
1 litre/1 3/4 pints Fish Stock (see page 00)
500g/1lb okra, sliced diagonally
175ml/6fl oz light beer
4 cloves
1 small sprig of thyme, leaves stripped off
2 tbs chopped spring onions

• Preheat the oven to 220°C/425°F/gas 7. Toast the cumin seeds on a baking sheet for a few minutes, then remove.
• Coat the prawns in a mixture of the paprika, salt and pepper, a little of the chopped garlic, half the lime juice and half the olive oil. Dry-fry them for a couple of minutes on each side until nicely browned, or better still, cook on a char-grill or barbecue. Put to one side.
• Heat the remaining olive oil in a large, heavy pan. Fry the bacon or pork belly until slightly browned, then add the chillies, shallots, cumin and remaining garlic. Turn the heat down and fry slowly for another 10 minutes. Meanwhile, heat up the stock in a separate pan.
• Add the tomatoes – they will start to break down almost immediately. Add the fish stock, okra, beer, cloves and the thyme. Simmer the soup for half an hour, then pour in the rest of the lime juice. Arrange the prawns on top, sprinkle with the spring onions and serve.
SERVES 4 [G]

NIGERIAN YAM SOUP

The yam is faintly alarming in appearance, not unlike a stray, unidentifiable portion of elephant. Its flesh is similar to the sweet potato, which can be used in this recipe if yams prove elusive. Either way, you will end up with a delicious, medium hot, thick yellow soup, which has been taken from *The Flavours of Africa Cookbook*, like its companion on this page.

50ml/2fl oz peanut oil

150g/5oz onion, chopped

125g/4oz carrot, chopped

4 jalapeño or serrano chillies, deseeded and chopped

250g/8oz tomatoes, chopped

750g/1¹/₂lb yam or sweet potato, peeled and cut into 2.5cm/1in cubes

250g/8oz potatoes, peeled and cut into 2.5cm/1in cubes

900ml/1¹/₂ pints Beef Stock (see page 148)

Salt and freshly ground black pepper

125ml/4fl oz double cream

Chopped parsley and grated root ginger, to garnish

• Heat the oil in a large, heavy pan, add the onion and carrot and fry gently for 2–3 minutes. Add the chillies, tomatoes, yam and potatoes and toss for 2–3 minutes. Heat the stock in a separate pan.
• Add the stock to the vegetables, season and bring to the boil. Reduce the heat, cover and simmer for 30 minutes. Allow to cool for 20 minutes, then blend in a food processor.
• Return the soup to the pan and bring back to the boil, then reduce the heat and add the cream in a steady stream, stirring constantly. Garnish with chopped parsley and grated ginger and serve.

SERVES 4-6 [G][N]

CURRIED CHICKEN AND BANANA SOUP

Or *Supa ya n dizi* as they call this fine stew in its native Tanzania. The curry powder it contains may come as a bit of a surprise, but then the Tanzanians have been trading with Asia for centuries. This recipe demonstrates the widely overlooked wisdom of combining chicken with bananas.

3 tbs peanut oil

2kg/4lb chicken, cut into pieces

3 cloves garlic, chopped

200g/7oz onions, chopped

200g/7oz celery, chopped

2¹/₂ tbs hot Madras curry powder

1¹/₂ tsp salt

1 tsp ground black pepper

1 tbs deseeded, chopped red chilli

1.8 litres/3 pints Chicken Stock (see page 147)

425g/14oz tomatoes, chopped

1 x 400g/14oz tin of coconut milk

2 slightly under-ripe bananas, thinly sliced

Chopped coriander, to garnish

• Heat the oil in a large, heavy pan. Brown the chicken pieces in the oil, then remove with a slotted spoon and reserve.
• Add the garlic, onion and celery and fry for 2–3 minutes, then add the curry powder, salt, pepper and chilli and fry for another 1–2 minutes, stirring to absorb the curry powder. Meanwhile, heat up the stock in a separate pan.
• Add the chicken pieces, stock, tomatoes and coconut, bring to the boil, then cover and simmer for about 40 minutes, until the chicken is meltingly tender.
• Take the chicken off the bone, add the bananas, and simmer for a further 10 minutes. Serve garnished with the chopped coriander.

SERVES 6 [D][G][N]

SWEET POTATO AND ROAST CASHEW SOUP

Cashew nuts are not cheap because of the way they grow, like a tiny quotation mark attached to the base of an orange-sized fruit body. They do, however, combine extraordinarily well with starchy sweet potatoes in this wonderfully filling African soup.

• Put the sweet potatoes and vegetable stock in a pan and boil for 15 minutes. Melt the butter in a large pan, add the chillies, ginger, garlic, carrots and onions and fry over moderate heat until soft. Mix in the flour with a wooden spoon.
• Pour in the stock and sweet potatoes, then blend in a food processor until smooth. Return to the pan and cook on low heat for 15 minutes, adding half the soy sauce, all the coconut milk and the coriander and seasoning at the last minute.
• Preheat the oven to 200°C/400°F/gas 6. Pour the remaining soy sauce over the cashew nuts in a shallow bowl, and mix thoroughly until they are all coated. Bake for about 10 minutes, turning them over continuously to ensure they are browned evenly and don't stick together.
• Serve the soup with a garnish of coriander leaves and the cashews sprinkled on top.
SERVES 4-6 [N][V]

500g/1lb sweet potatoes, sliced
1 litre/1¾ pints Vegetable Stock (see page 147)
25g/1oz butter
1 tsp chopped red chillies (more if you dare)
1 tbs chopped root ginger
1 tbs chopped garlic
175g/6oz carrots, sliced
175g/6oz onions, sliced
50g/2oz plain flour
3 tbs soy sauce
175ml/6fl oz coconut milk
A few sprigs of coriander, plus extra for garnish
Salt and white pepper
250g/8oz cashew nuts

CALLALOO WITH CRAB AND PORK

1 kg/2lb small live soup
    crabs, or regular crab
1.25 litres/2 pints Fish
    Stock (see page 149)
150g/5oz pork belly,
    chopped into 1cm/
    ½in cubes
25g/1oz butter
1 onion, chopped
3 cloves garlic, chopped
1–2 red chillies, chopped
½ tsp ground cinnamon
¼ tsp ground nutmeg
175g/6oz okra, chopped
4 allspice berries
1 sprig of thyme
500g/1lb fresh spinach,
    chopped
300ml/½ pint coconut
    milk (fresh for
    maximum authenticity)
2 tbs lime juice
Soy sauce, to taste
4 spring onions, chopped

Callaloo is a generic term for the green leaves of plants grown in the Caribbean such as eddoe, coco, taro and dasheen. As none of these are widely available in the West, we've used spinach in the recipe below. Johnny was once served a bowl of this on the slopes of Blue Mountain Peak in Jamaica, shortly before the entire village broke out into a mass machete brawl, forcing him to beat a hasty retreat. It didn't put him off this fabulous soup though. Soup crabs are little, green and French and can be ordered from good fishmongers. If they are unavailable, use ordinary crab.

• Place the soup crabs and stock in a large pan over medium heat. Simmer for 20 minutes, then remove the crabs and pound until completely mashed. Put them back in the stock and simmer for another 10 minutes then remove and strain through a conical sieve. This should separate the crab meat from the shell fragments. Put the crab meat aside, discard the shells, and put the stock back on low heat to stay warm.
• Fry the pork belly in its own fat in a large pan until crispy, remove with a slotted spoon and set aside. Add the butter to the pork fat in the pan and fry the onion, garlic, chillies, cinnamon and nutmeg in it for a few minutes. Add the fish stock, okra, allspice berries and thyme and simmer for 20 minutes or so. The okra should thicken the soup slightly.
• Add the spinach and let it cook down for a minute or so. Then add the coconut milk, lime juice, reserved crab meat and a little soy sauce to taste. Serve sprinkled with the crispy pork and top with the chopped spring onions.
SERVES 4-6 [G][N]

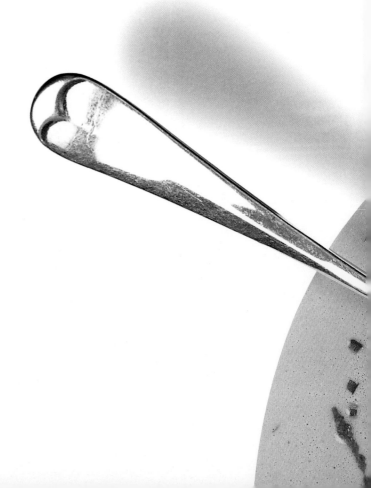

ZIMBABWEAN PEANUT AND RED PEPPER STEW

Zimbabwe is landlocked, but this doesn't prevent the population from having a tremendous appetite for prawns and shrimps imported from neighbouring Mozambique. Dried shrimps make a critical contribution to this earthy stew.

- Preheat the oven to 220°C/425°F/gas 7. Place the peanuts in a roasting tin, pour the soy sauce, honey and sesame oil over them and roast for 5-8 minutes, turning frequently to prevent them burning. Remove and reserve.
- Roast the peppers for 30 minutes. Skin, core, deseed and slice them. Reserve.
- Heat the oil in a large, heavy pan over moderate heat. Add the onion, ginger, garlic, shrimps and chillies, cover and sweat for 5 minutes. Heat up the stock in a separate pan. Add the stock, bay leaves, thyme and sweet potatoes to the pan and simmer for 20 minutes or so, until the sweet potatoes are cooked. Remove the bay and thyme, stir in the peanut butter and tomato purée, and blend the stew in a food processor until smooth.
- Return the soup to the pan over heat, add the red peppers and simmer for 2–3 minutes. Serve garnished with the spring onions and the roasted peanuts.

SERVES 4-6 [G][N]

125g/4oz peanuts
1 tsp soy sauce
1 tsp honey
1/2 tsp sesame oil
2 red peppers
25ml/1fl oz olive oil
150g/5oz onion, chopped
1 tsp chopped root ginger
2 cloves garlic, chopped
2 red chillies, chopped and
  deseeded
1.25 litres/2 pints Chicken or
  Vegetable Stock (see page
  147)
2 bay leaves
1 sprig of thyme
300g/10oz sweet potato,
  peeled and chopped
200g/7oz smooth peanut butter
  1 tbs tomato purée
    2 spring onions, chopped

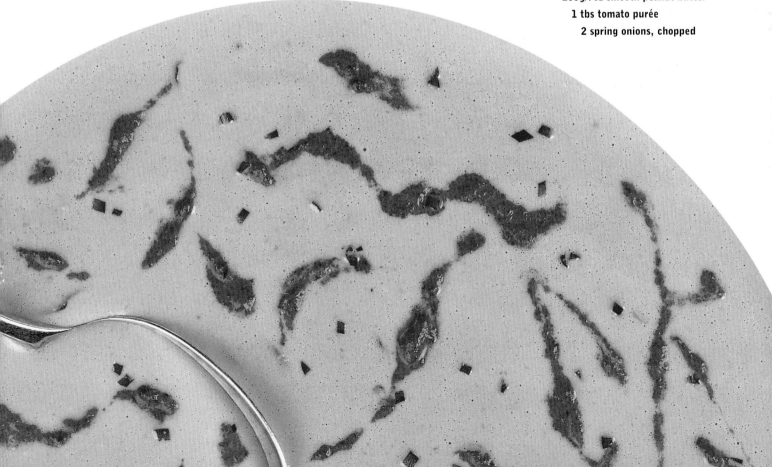

JERK CHICKEN SOUP WITH PUMPKIN

THE MARINADE

125ml/4fl oz orange juice

125ml/4fl oz balsamic
  vinegar

125ml/4fl oz white wine
  vinegar

4 tbs olive oil

2 tbs soy sauce

1/2 tsp cayenne pepper

2 tsp whole allspice

1/2 tsp cinnamon

1 tsp paprika

1 sprig of oregano

2 tsp brown sugar

1 tsp fennel seed

1 tsp chopped root ginger

2 cloves garlic, chopped

1/2 tsp black pepper

1/2 tsp ground nutmeg

1 sprig of thyme

2 shallots, roughly chopped

2 bay leaves

2 scotch bonnet peppers,
  deseeded and chopped

THE SOUP

300g/10oz chicken fillets

2 tbs olive oil

175g/6oz onion, chopped

125g/4oz celery, chopped

1 litre/1²/3 pints Chicken
  Stock (see page 147)

50g/2oz plain flour

175ml/6fl oz passata

1 small pumpkin,
  peeled, de-
  seeded, cut
  into cubes

4 spring onions,
  chopped

1 sprig of parsley

One of our most satisfying experiences has been the creation of delicious soups based on classic non-soup recipes; this is a prime example.

In seventeenth-century Jamaica, the runaway slaves who came to be known as the Maroons invented an ingenious method of preserving their meat, known as 'jerking'. First the meat (usually chicken or pork) was marinated in a fiery concoction of wild herbs and spices. Then it was barbecued over pimento wood (from the allspice tree) in subterranean pits.

The recipe below involves the happy marriage of jerk chicken and pumpkin, a vegetable which readily absorbs its partner's spicy essence. The scorching scotch bonnet peppers are essential, but require cautious handling, lest they overwhelm this beautifully exotic soup.

• Blend the ingredients for the marinade in a food processor. Thinly slice the chicken and put it in a bowl, pour on the marinade and turn to coat well. Cover and leave in the fridge for up to 48 hours (the longer the better).

• Heat the olive oil in a heavy-bottomed pan, add the onion and celery and fry until slightly browned. Remove the chicken from the marinade and char-grill on both sides until cooked. Add the marinade to the pan and cook on medium heat for 5 minutes, stirring to prevent it sticking to the bottom. Meanwhile, heat up the chicken stock in a separate pan.

• Add the flour and passata to the pan, cook for a minute or two, then gradually whisk in the stock. Add the pumpkin and cook on low to medium heat until the pumpkin becomes semi-translucent (adding water or more stock if the mixture becomes too thick). Add the chicken, spring onions and parsley and heat through.

SERVES 6 [L][D]

PLANTAIN, CHICKEN AND CORN

Plantains are large cooking bananas. For this recipe, you will want them green, or just starting to turn yellow. Any yellower and the soup will be too sweet. This soup looks attractive with chunks of charred corn shaved off the cob lying on its surface.

6 corn-on-the-cob
125g/4oz butter
250g/8oz shallots, chopped
2 medium hot red chillies, deseeded and chopped
4 cloves garlic, chopped
1.25 litres/2 pints Chicken Stock (see page 147)
1 medium butternut squash, deseeded and chopped
2 plantains, peeled and chopped
Salt and freshly ground black pepper
175ml/6fl oz coconut milk
375g/12oz chicken fillet, cut into chunks
1 sprig of thyme
Spring onions, chopped, to garnish

• Brush the corn on the cob with a little of the butter with a pinch of the chilli and garlic mixed in. Grill or bake in a hot oven (230°C/45°F/gas 8) until they brown – about 20 minutes if baking. Shave off the corn in chunks with a sharp knife.
• Melt the remaining butter in a large, heavy pan, add the shallots, chillies and garlic and fry gently until softened. Heat up the stock in a separate pan. Add the stock, squash and plantain and simmer for at least half an hour. You will notice the starches from the plantain thickening up the soup nicely. Add salt and pepper to taste, then blend in a food processor.
• Return the soup to the pan, add the coconut milk, chicken and thyme and simmer for 5 minutes, or until the chicken is cooked. Adjust the seasoning and pour into bowls, laying the corn on top, browned side up. Garnish with spring onions and serve.
SERVES 4-6 [N]

RED CHILLI PAPAYA

This extremely funky South African soup can be served either hot or cold, and can be more or less fierce depending on the chillies you use. We suggest using slightly unripe papayas (or pawpaws as old-timers and colonial types tend to call them) to impart a more savoury taste. Papayas grow like a weed in the tropics – Nick's Malaysian girlfriend threw some seeds out of the window as a small girl and now has a papaya forest in the family backyard. The inspiration for this recipe came from *The Flavours of Africa Cookbook*.

25g/1oz butter
175g/6oz onion, chopped
1/2 tsp finely chopped root ginger
1 tbs chopped, deseeded red chillies
3 large papayas, peeled, deseeded and chopped
175ml/6fl oz papaya or mango juice
Salt and white pepper
Pinch of ground mace
600ml/1 pint milk
600ml/1 pint Vegetable Stock (see page 147)
2 tsp cornflour
175ml/6fl oz double cream

• Melt the butter in a large, heavy pan. Add the onions and fry gently with the ginger until soft. Add the chillies, papaya, juice, salt, pepper and mace and simmer until pulpy (about 20 minutes), then blend in a food processor. Return to the pan, add the milk and stock and simmer for a few minutes.
• Whisk the cornflour into the cream, then pour the mixture into the soup, whisking all the time. Adjust the seasoning and serve immediately, or chill in the fridge.
SERVES 4-6 [V]

ROASTED CORN SOUP WITH CORN BREAD

THE BREAD

2 eggs, lightly beaten

200ml/7fl oz sour cream

400ml/14fl oz creamed
  corn

1 onion, grated

300g/10oz yellow cornmeal

2 tsp baking powder

1 tsp salt

Vegetable oil

200g/7oz grated Cheddar
  cheese

THE SOUP

25g/1oz small dried
  shrimps

1 tsp cumin seed

1 tbs chopped coriander

2 cloves garlic

2 red chillies, deseeded

2 shallots, sliced

1 red pepper, roasted (see
  page 156), skinned,
  cored and deseeded

50g/2oz butter

200ml/7fl oz coconut milk

1.25 litres/2 pints Chicken
  or Vegetable Stock (see
  page 147)

Salt and freshly ground
  black pepper

Pinch of ground nutmeg

6 corn-on-the-cob, roasted
  or barbecued, kernels
  shaved off the cob

In Southern Africa, the dietary importance of corn-on-the-cob or maize is such that the locals simply call it 'mealie'. In the Caribbean, meanwhile, 'corn' is a slang term for money. Johnny's uncle grew up in Zimbabwe, but now lives in rural Essex. One summer, to his delight, maize started sprouting in the field next to his house. Not being what you'd call a master chef, he quite happily lived on nothing else for weeks. He'd have been even chirpier, though, if he had known how to make this great, nourishing soup. The cornbread recipe comes courtesy of Lee Bailey's *Country Weekend*.

• Preheat the oven to 200°C/400°F/gas 6. To make the corn bread, mix together the eggs, cream, creamed corn and onion. In another bowl, mix the cornmeal, baking powder and salt, and then combine with the creamed corn mixture.

• Brush a 23cm/9in round baking tin with oil. Pour in half the batter, then sprinkle 2/3 of the cheddar on top. Pour in the rest of the batter, and sprinkle the remaining cheese on top. Bake in the oven for 30-35 minutes.

• To make the soup, blend the shrimps, cumin seeds, coriander, garlic, chillies, shallots and red pepper in a food processor. Melt the butter in a large, heavy pan, add the mixture and simmer gently. Add the coconut milk, stock, seasonings, nutmeg and half the corn kernels and gently bring to the boil. Blend in a food processor, return the soup to the pan, and simmer for a few more minutes with the rest of the corn kernels. Serve with the warm corn bread.

SERVES 4-6 [N][OPTIONALLY V]

ITAL RUNDOWN WITH PLANTAIN CHIPS

THE SAUCE

600ml/1 pint coconut milk

125g/4oz onion

2 cloves garlic, chopped

1 sprig of thyme

1 sprig of parsley

2 cloves

1/2 tsp ground cinnamon

1 tsp chopped root ginger

1 tsp deseeded and
  chopped red chilli

THE VEGETABLES

1 tbs olive oil

175g/6oz carrots, chopped

375g/12oz cabbage,
  shredded

1 red pepper, chopped,
  cored and deseeded

2 corn-on-the-cob, kernels
  shaved off

200ml/7fl oz water

3 spring onions, chopped,
  to garnish

THE PLANTAIN CHIPS

1 green plantain, peeled
  and very thinly sliced

250ml/8fl oz vegetable oil

This recipe has been adapted from a recipe of Rosamund Grant's. To the strictest adherents of Rastafarianism, Ital is the equivalent of kosher. Ital cooking is completely vegetarian and salt-free. As a result, it is exceptionally healthy – Jamaica's hardcore Rastas certainly look good on it, despite (or they would say because of) their copious and sacramental consumption of ganja. Rundown is a method of reducing coconut milk to a delectable thick, creamy sauce, while plantains are large cooking bananas, available in African and Caribbean grocery stores. This is more of a stew than a soup, but too good to miss.

• To make the sauce, place all the ingredients in a pan and simmer until it thickens, taking care not to let it boil.
• Heat the olive oil in a large frying pan, add all the vegetables and fry gently for a few minutes. Add the water, and cook for a further 5 minutes before adding the rundown sauce. Stir well and cook for another few minutes.
• Meanwhile, to make the chips, heat the oil in a frying pan and fry the plantain slices over moderate heat until golden brown. Remove with a slotted spoon and drain on kitchen paper. Serve on top of the vegetables with a sprinkling of spring onion.

SERVES 4 [V][L][D][N]

Fusion

IN A SENSE, the whole story of soup has been one of fusion. From the moment the first caravans began to ply the spice routes of the ancient world, people have been irresistably tempted to throw a handful of some exotic new ingredient into their stockpots just to see what would happen. Soup has been in a constant state of evolution ever since, endlessly responding to cultural exchanges brought about by wars, conquests, voyages of discovery and the migration of peoples. Some of the best results have already appeared in this book, from the Anglo-Indian mulligatawny to the gamut of European soups that depend on New World ingredients for their very existence.

In recent years, however, the term 'fusion' has become particularly associated with a style of cooking that marries the flavours and techniques of the Orient with those of the West. If there is mayonnaise in your sushi roll for instance, you're eating fusion (and probably horrifying the older generation of Japanese while you're at it). Often described as East-West cuisine, fusion cooking is very much a product of the jet age. In a world where you are as likely to find the citizens of Bangkok dining out on pasta and enchiladas as you are to find their counterparts in Bognor Regis tucking into curries and noodles, fusion cuisine is the realization of an historical inevitability.

If the old fusion cooking was premised on ideas and ingredients scuttling to and fro across the Atlantic, the new fusion is very much focused on those countries which border the Pacific (hence the alternative description, 'Pacific Rim' cuisine). Urban centres such as Seattle, Sydney and Singapore are at the heart of this foody revolution, synthesizing vibrant tastes from the previously discrete culinary traditions of

Thailand, China, Japan and the Americas. A dash of Old Europe is often thrown in for good measure, transformed by the judicious substitution of Eastern ingredients for tired old Western ones (the recipe below for cream of shiitake mushroom soup is a case in point). The keynotes of fusion cooking are freshness, inventiveness and flavour. It is a global village out there, and fusion cooking is taking full advantage.

A word of warning. The individual cuisines at the heart of fusion cooking have evolved an integrity over a long, long period that must be respected. The authentic must be mastered before you can expect much joy with the experimental – it is no good for instance chucking star anise and lemon grass willy-nilly into European classics and expecting guaranteed results. But with the basic grounding and global overview we hope this book will have given you, you should be well set to carry out successful fusion experiments of your own. In the meantime, the soups that follow will give you a taste of the most dynamic and inspirational area of cooking in the world today.

SPICY LOBSTER BISQUE

The recipe for this luxurious Thai/European hybrid somewhat surprisingly reached us via Canada, by way of Claudine, our former sous chef.

2 raw, medium sized lobsters, either live or frozen

1.1 litres/2 pints Fish Stock (see page 149)

300g/10oz potato, cut into small chunks

125g/4oz carrot

50g/2oz onion

50g/2oz celery

1 tsp finely chopped red chilli

2 tsp finely chopped ginger

1 tsp chopped garlic

50g/2oz butter

6 shredded kaffir lime leaves

2 blades lemon grass, finely chopped

a couple of pinches of saffron strands

200ml/7fl oz dark beer

2 tbs soy sauce

1 tbs nam pla

250ml/9fl oz passata

125ml/4fl oz cream

2 tbs chopped coriander to garnish

- Simmer the lobsters in the fish stock for 20 minutes, then remove them and break off the tails. Remove, chop and reserve the meat from the tails, then pummel the shells (legs and all) with a rolling pin and place them back in the stock, and simmer for a further 20 minutes.
- Boil the potato chunks for about 15 minutes in slightly salted water, drain and reserve.
- Chop the carrot, onion and celery, and fry them with the chilli, ginger and garlic in the butter over a moderate heat for about 10 minutes, until soft. Strain in the hot fish and lobster stock through a conical sieve, discarding the shells and legs.
- Add the lime leaves, lemon grass, saffron, beer, soy and fish sauces, passata and potato chunks and simmer for 10 minutes before plending in a food processor.
- Finish the soup off by adding the cream, bringing the soup to boiling point and garnishing.

SERVES 4-6 [G]

MELON AND GINGER WITH GLASS NOODLES

This tangy, delectable soup is refreshing writ large, with the glass noodles nicely complementing the translucency of the melon. Melons come in all shapes and sizes – ogens, canteloupes, honeydews, galias, piel de sapo and watermelon. We like to use a selection. If, for some reason you anticipate a blazing row during the meal, leave out the watermelon as it contains an enzyme which reacts badly with human anger, leading to heartburn.

Juice from the excess melon pulp, passed through a muslin cloth

250ml/8fl oz dry white wine

175ml/6fl oz grape juice

Juice of 1 lime

Caster sugar, to taste

800g/1lb 10oz melon balls (use a Parisian baller if available)

125g/4oz medium glass noodles, cooked and chilled in cold water

Sprig of mint

1 tsp finely shredded root ginger

- Mix together the melon juice, white wine, grape and lime juices. Taste and add a little sugar if you find it needs sweetening.
- The next bit resembles the construction of some kind of deranged wig. Half fill each bowl with the juice, then add a couple of melon balls, a few strands of noodles, some more balls, some more noodles, and so on. Finally garnish with mint leaves and the finely shredded ginger.

SERVES 4-6 [V][L][D][G]

CREAM OF SHIITAKE MUSHROOM

Shiitake mushrooms are incredibly flavoursome, perhaps because they are grown on logs of oak. They also contain a substance which helps to lower blood cholesterol levels, just as well given the plentiful double cream in the recipe. This soup makes it into the Fusion chapter simply because shiitake mushrooms are a Japanese gift to the culinary world.

500g/1lb new
   potatoes, diced
Salt and freshly
   ground black pepper
50g/2oz butter
125g/4oz carrot, sliced
125g/4oz leek, sliced
125g/4oz celery, sliced
125g/4oz onion, sliced
300g/10oz chestnut
   mushrooms, sliced
1.25 litres/2 pints
   Chicken or
   Vegetable Stock (see
   page 147)
50g/2oz plain flour
250g/8oz fresh shiitake
   mushrooms, thinly
   sliced
250ml/8fl oz cream
1 tbs soy sauce
1 tbs chopped tarragon
Dash of medium sherry
   (optional)

• Boil the new potatoes in salted water for 10 minutes, until almost cooked. Drain and reserve.
• Melt the butter in a large, heavy pan. Add the carrot, leek, celery, onion and chestnut mushrooms and fry gently until soft, about 5 minutes. Meanwhile, heat up the stock to simmering point in a separate pan. Add the flour to the vegetables and stir well until absorbed.
• Pour in the hot stock and bring to the boil. Turn the heat down and simmer for 2–3 minutes. Add the new potatoes and the shiitake mushrooms and simmer for 5–10 minutes, stirring frequently.
• To finish the soup, add the cream, soy sauce and tarragon, and season to taste. A dash of sherry wouldn't go amiss.
SERVES 4-6 [OPTIONALLY V]

SWEET POTATO, COCONUT AND CHICKEN

When Nick finally turns up his toes, they will probably engrave this recipe on his tombstone. We sell more chicken, sweet potato and coconut soup than anything else. It is only with the greatest reluctance that we divulge the secret formula here.

50g/2oz butter
125g/4oz carrot, sliced
125g/4oz leek, sliced
125g/4oz celery, sliced
125g/4oz onion, sliced
1 tsp chopped red
   chilli
1 tsp chopped root
   ginger
3 cloves garlic,
   chopped
1.25 litres/2 pints
   Chicken Stock (see
   page 147)
50g/2oz plain flour
600g/1¼lb sweet
   potato, cubed
500g/1lb chicken
   breast, sliced
1 tbs chopped
   coriander
1 tbs chopped spring
   onion
Soy sauce, to taste
1 x 400g/14oz tin of
   coconut milk

• Melt the butter in a large, heavy pan. Add the carrot, leek, celery, onion, chilli, ginger and garlic and fry gently until soft, about 5 minutes. Meanwhile, heat up the stock in a separate pan. Add the flour to the vegetables and stir until well absorbed, then whisk in the stock gradually.
• Add the sweet potatoes, bring to the boil, then cover and simmer for about 20 minutes, or until the sweet potatoes are cooked.
• Blend the soup in a food processor, return to the pan over low heat, and add the chicken, coriander, spring onion, soy sauce and coconut milk. Simmer for 5 minutes and serve.
SERVES 4-6 [N]

ROASTED PEPPER SOUP WITH GINGER AND SCALLOPS

6 red peppers, roasted,
   skinned, cored and
   deseeded
3 tbs olive oil
1 tsp paprika
50g/2oz white breadcrumbs
3 tbs balsamic vinegar
Salt and freshly ground
   black pepper
450ml/3/4 pint Fish Stock
   (see page 149)
8 large scallops (coral
   optional)
1 tsp finely chopped root
   ginger
1 tsp finely chopped garlic
25g/1oz butter
2 tsp lime juice
Coriander sprigs, to garnish

Sweet, delicate scallops somehow manage to combine with considerably perkier ingredients without being in the least overwhelmed in this fine cold soup. It is a moot point whether or not to include the scallop coral (the vaguely triangular orange bit) – some love it, others find it a little bitter. We've left it optional. As this soup is quite rich, you may want to serve it in small portions.

• In a food processor blend the peppers, olive oil, paprika, breadcrumbs, balsamic vinegar, a little salt and pepper and the fish stock until smooth. Adjust the seasoning to taste and put in the fridge.
• Season the scallops with salt and pepper, the garlic and a little of the ginger. Melt the butter in a frying pan or griddle pan and cook the scallops for 2 minutes on each side. Just before you take them off, pour the lime juice on top and let it sizzle for a few seconds.
• Portion out the soup into bowls, placing 2 scallops on top of each. Garnish with the rest of the ginger and the coriander.

SERVES 4

BUTTERNUT SQUASH WITH ROASTED PEPPER

50g/2oz walnuts, chopped

1 tsp soy sauce

1 tsp honey

2 medium butternut
squash

2 green cooking apples,
peeled, halved and
cored

50g/2oz butter

125g/4oz carrot, chopped

125g/4oz onion, chopped

50g/2oz celery, chopped

1/2 tsp ground cinnamon

50g/2oz plain flour

1.25 litres/2 pints Chicken
or Vegetable Stock (see
page 147)

Salt and white pepper

Pinch each of chopped
rosemary and oregano

2 red peppers, roasted,
skinned, cored,
deseeded and finely
shredded

125ml/4fl oz double cream

This soup is sweet, delicious, and a mite unusual. Butternut squash is a full-tasting vegetable, but quite mild, so you need a lot of it for the taste to really come out. Chicken stock makes the whole thing tastier, but vegetarians among you will know what to do…

• Preheat the oven to 220°C/425°F/gas 7. Place the walnuts on a baking tray, coat them with the soy sauce and honey and bake for 5 minutes. Remove from the heat and leave to cool. Leave the oven at the same temperature.
• Cut the butternut squash in half lengthways, remove the seeds with a spoon, and place face down in a roasting tin with the apples. Add 1cm/1/2in of water and cook in the preheated oven until soft, about half an hour. If the apples become soft before the squash, remove them. When both are ready, scoop out the butternut flesh and place in a bowl with the apples.
• Melt the butter in a large pan. Add the carrot, onion and celery and fry with the cinnamon until soft. Mix in the flour. Heat up the stock in a separate pan and add it to the vegetables, whisking it in to break up any lumps. Add the butternut squash/apple mixture, simmer for 5 minutes, then blend in a food processor.
• Season to taste, add the herbs, and finish off by stirring in the peppers and cream. Garnish with the sweet-coated walnuts.
SERVES 4-6 [N][OPTIONALLY V]

TORTILLA SOUP WITH CHICKEN WONTONS

THE WONTONS
125g/4oz minced chicken
2 spring onions, finely
    chopped
½ tsp finely chopped root
    ginger
1 tbs soy sauce
1 tsp sesame oil
1 packet wanton wrappers
1 egg, lightly whisked

THE SOUP
125g/4oz pinto beans,
    or a mixture of dried
    beans, soaked overnight
    and drained
2 tbs olive oil
1 tsp cumin seeds
2 cloves garlic,
    chopped
150g/5oz onion, chopped
6 tomatoes, skinned,
    deseeded and chopped
200ml/7fl oz passata
2 bay leaves
1 sprig of thyme
1.25 litres/2 pints Chicken
    Stock
    (see page 147)
soy sauce, to taste

THE GARNISH
4 corn tortillas
vegetable oil for deep-
    frying
Sea salt
50g/2oz grated Cheddar
    cheese

Mexico meets China in this one, deep-fried corn tortilla strips providing an interesting textural contrast to the wontons. Wonton skins are widely available in Oriental supermarkets, as we've mentioned before. Chef Suki at Mason's gave us the inspiration for this recipe, which comes from *East West Food.*

• Boil the beans in plenty of water for about 1½ hours or until soft. Drain and reserve.
• To make the wontons, mix the minced chicken, spring onions, ginger, soy sauce and sesame oil thoroughly in a bowl. Place a small blob of this mixture in each wonton skin, paint the edges with the egg and pinch together to form sealed parcels. Reserve in the fridge.
• Heat the olive oil in a large pan over a medium heat. Add the cumin and fry for 1 minute. Add the garlic and onions and cook until soft. Then add the tomatoes and cook until they are mushy. Add the passata, bay leaves, thyme, stock and the pinto beans, plus soy sauce to taste, and simmer for 20 minutes.
• Meanwhile, cut the tortillas into strips and deep-fry in the oil until crisp and golden brown. Drain on kitchen paper, sprinkle with sea salt and reserve.
• Drop the wontons into the simmering soup. When they rise to the surface, they are cooked and the soup is ready to serve. Garnish with the deep-fried tortilla strips and sprinkle with grated cheese.

SERVES 4

CHILLED AVOCADO LIME

You need a rich chicken stock to bring out the flavour of this thick, cold, lime-green soup, as Nick has discovered while wiling away the hours in his friend Jamie's house in Mexico. It goes particularly well with hot garlic bread. *Terrific Pacific* by Anya von Gremzen and John Welchman was the inspiration for both the recipes on this page.

5 ripe, medium
   avocados
1 litre/1¾ pints
   Chicken Stock (see
   page 147)
3 cloves garlic
Juice of 2 limes
4 red chillies,
   deseeded and
   chopped
2 slices stale white
   bread
5 medium tomatoes,
   skinned, deseeded
   and chopped
1 medium red onion,
   finely chopped
1 bunch coriander,
   chopped
Salt and freshly
   ground black pepper
Zest of 1 lime
4 spring onions,
   chopped

• Scoop the flesh out of the avocados. If not using immediately, cover with lime juice and refrigerate with clingfilm touching the surface to prevent browning.
• Blend the avocados, chicken stock, garlic, lime juice, chillies and bread in a food processor.
• Add the chopped tomatoes, onion and coriander, season to taste and mix thoroughly. Serve with the lime zest and the chopped spring onions sprinkled on top.

SERVES 4-6 [L]

CUCUMBER AND MANGO BISQUE

Cucumbers and mangoes are just about the most refreshing vegetables and fruits in existence. Make sure you pick ripe but firm examples for this exquisite chilled soup, or it might become a little on the watery side.

2 large mangoes,
   peeled, chopped and
   puréed
425g/14oz cucumber,
   peeled, deseeded
   and chopped
125ml/4fl oz single
   cream
200ml/7fl oz Chicken
   or Vegetable Stock
   (see page 147)
125ml/4fl oz Greek
   yoghurt
1 clove garlic, chopped
2 mild red chillies,
   deseeded and
   chopped
1 small bunch basil,
   chopped
1 tbs balsamic vinegar
Juice of 1 lemon
A little salt, to taste
Diced mango and
   cucumber plus a few
   basil leaves, to
   garnish

• Put all the ingredients except the salt in a food processor and blend. Add salt to taste.
• Chill in the fridge, then serve garnished with small dice of mango and cucumber and a few basil leaves.

SERVES 4 [G][OPTIONALLY V]

LAMB AND AUBERGINE WITH NOODLES

This rich, thin soup is a winner, marrying Oriental flavours with ingredients frankly more typical of Greece. Such is the beauty of fusion cooking...

2 medium aubergines
50ml/2fl oz olive oil
Salt and freshly
    ground black pepper
1.25 litres/2 pints
    Lamb Stock (see
    page 149)
2 tbs soy sauce
2 red chillies, de-
    seeded and roughly
    chopped
5 spring onions, sliced
1 tsp chopped root
    ginger
500g/1lb lamb fillet,
    very thinly sliced
500g/1lb pak choi
300g/10oz fresh egg
    noodles
Coriander leaves, to
    garnish

• Preheat the oven to 230C/450F/gas 8. Cut the aubergines in half lengthways and place in a roasting tin cut side up. Brush with the olive oil, sprinkle with salt and black pepper and roast in the hot oven for 20–25 minutes until nice and brown on top. Leave to cool, slice into sections and reserve.
• Heat up the lamb stock in a large pan until it boils, then reduce to a simmer. Add the soy sauce, chillies, spring onions and ginger, and simmer for 2–3 minutes.
• Add the lamb, pak choi and aubergine and simmer for a few more minutes. Meanwhile, cook the egg noodles for 3–4 minutes in boiling water, then refresh in cold water.
• Serve the soup on a bed of noodles and garnish with a few coriander leaves.

SERVES 4 [D]

CREAM OF PUMPKIN WITH COCONUT

The grated coconut provides a pleasing contrast to the smooth texture of this delicately spiced soup, which we have adapted from one in *Terrific Pacific*.

50g/2oz butter
200g/7oz onion, sliced
125g/4oz carrot, sliced
125g/4oz celery, sliced
1 tsp chopped root
    ginger
1 tsp chopped garlic
1.25 litres/2 pints
    Vegetable Stock
    (see page 147)
800g/1¾lb pumpkin,
    peeled, diced and
    boiled until soft
1 x 400g/14oz tin of
    coconut milk
125ml/4fl oz double
    cream
Pinch of ground
    cinnamon
Pinch of ground
    nutmeg
Salt and freshly
    ground black pepper
1–2 tbs grated coconut
5 spring onions,
    chopped

• Melt the butter in a large pan. Add the onion, carrot, celery, ginger and garlic, cover and sweat for about 5 minutes, until soft. Add the vegetable stock and pumpkin, bring to the boil, then blend immediately in a food processor.
• Return the soup to the pan over low heat, add the coconut milk, cream, cinnamon, nutmeg, salt and pepper and simmer for 10 minutes.
• Serve sprinkled with the grated coconut and the spring onions.

SERVES 4-6 [N][V][G]

PEANUT AND CABBAGE

Not the most obvious combination, but an exceedingly effective one. With its Oriental feel, this soup is particularly delicious with fried pork and noodles.

25ml/1fl oz olive oil
1 tsp sesame oil
150g/5oz onion, sliced
125g/4oz celery, sliced
1 tsp chopped, deseeded red chilli
1 tsp chopped root ginger
3 cloves garlic, chopped
1.3 litres/21/3 pints Chicken Stock (see page 147)
250g/8oz potatoes, peeled and roughly chopped
200g/7oz smooth peanut butter
425g/14oz savoy cabbage, shredded
2 corn-on-the-cobs, kernels shaved off
1 tbs nam pla or nuoc mam (fish sauce)
1 tbs soy sauce
200g/7oz beansprouts
125g/4oz shelled, roasted peanuts, crushed

• Put the olive and sesame oils in a large pan, add the onion, carrot, celery, chilli, ginger and garlic, cover and sweat over a moderate heat for a few minutes. Heat up the stock in a seperate pan. Add the stock and the potatoes to the vegetables, bring to the boil, cover and simmer until the potatoes are soft, about 20 minutes.
• Add the peanut butter and blend thoroughly in a food processor. Return the soup to the pan over low heat, add the savoy cabbage, corn, nam pla and soy sauce, and simmer for 10 minutes.
• Serve garnished with beansprouts and the crushed, roasted peanuts.

SERVES 4-6 [L] [D] [G] [N]

SWEETCORN AND LEMONGRASS CHOWDER

This soup draws its sweetness from the sun drenched fields of the South of France and its bite from the tenements of downtown Bangkok.

35g unsalted butter (approx. 1 heaped tbp)
100g/31/2oz carrot sliced
100g/31/2oz celery, sliced
4 stalks lemongrass, finely chopped
1 tsp red chilli, chopped
1/2 teaspoon garlic, chopped
1 litre/13/4 pints chicken stock
250g/8oz potato, diced
100ml/31/2fl oz coconut milk
2 tbs fish sauce
120ml/33/4fl oz double cream
2 tsp cornflour
A sprig of coriander, chopped

• Gently fry the carrot, onion, lemongrass, chilli, ginger and garlic in the butter until soft.
• Add the chicken stock and potato and simmer for twenty minutes or until the potato is soft.
• Blend until smooth. Pass through a conical sieve and return to a clean pan.
• Add the coconut milk, fish sauce and double cream, then check your seasoning. You may want to add more fish sauce.
• Mix the cornflour with a few drops of water until dissolved, then pour into the soup, stirring constantly. You will find the soup thickens up immediately.
• Pour the soup into bowls and garnish with coriander.

SERVES 4 [v]